To Diane,

Toward a tempeh world!

♡ Seth

June 2021

IN SEARCH OF THE WILD

Tofurky

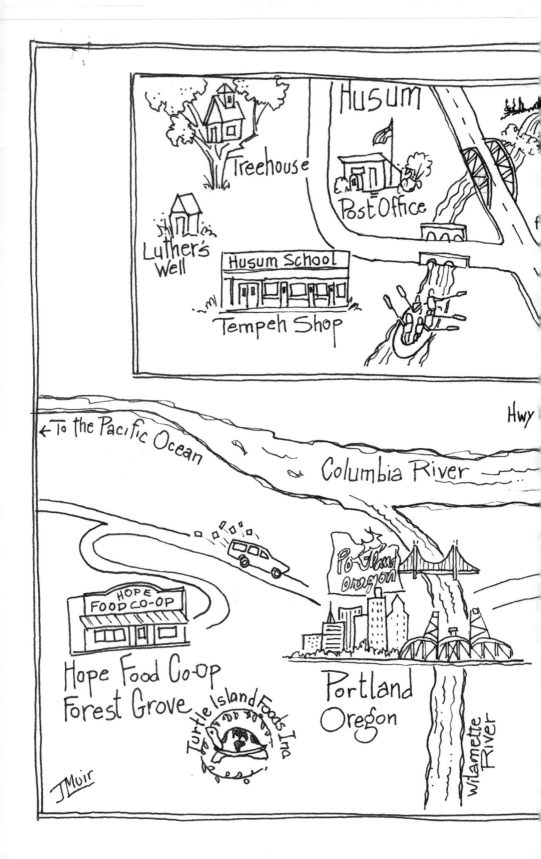

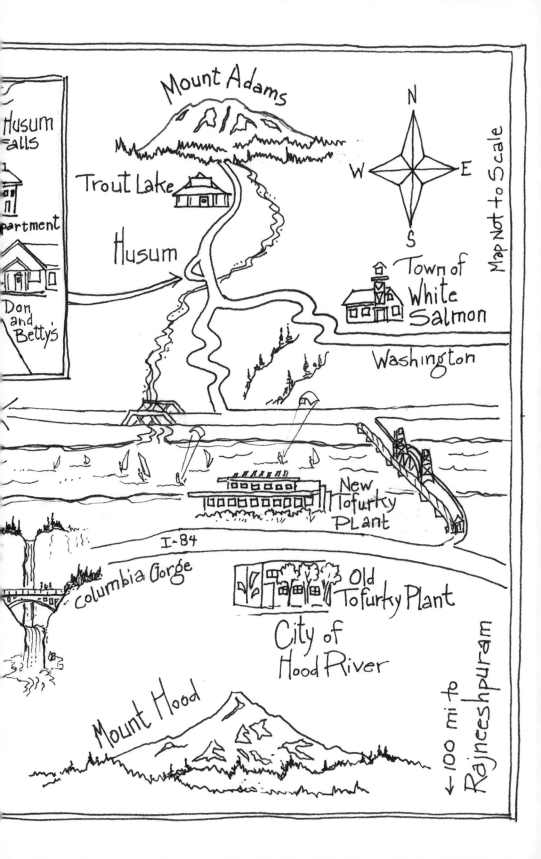

IN SEARCH OF THE WILD

Tofurky

HOW A BUSINESS MISFIT PIONEERED **PLANT-BASED FOODS** BEFORE THEY WERE COOL

SETH TIBBOTT

with Steve Richardson

DIVERSION
BOOKS

For more information, email info@diversionbooks.com

Diversion Books
A division of Diversion Publishing Corp.
443 Park Avenue South, suite 1004
New York, NY 10016
www.diversionbooks.com

Book design by Aubrey Khan, Neuwirth & Associates

First Diversion Books edition, April 2020
Hardcover ISBN: 978-1-63576-653-0
eBook ISBN: 978-1-63576-655-4

Printed in The United States of America

1 3 5 7 9 10 8 6 4 2

Library of Congress cataloging-in-publication data is available on file.

For my wife Sue, my brother Bob, and the many, many others who have helped me turn this wonderfully unrealistic dream into a great business. This would be a pretty sad story if you weren't in it.

CONTENTS

IN SEARCH OF THE WILD

Tofurky

INTRODUCTION

THIS MAY NOT BE THE
BOOK YOU'RE LOOKING FOR

This is the story of how I built The Tofurky Company—me and a host of amazing people. It's the story of this company's humble roots in my early years and its painfully slow growth through much of my adult life. For the longest time, I was sure that tempeh, tofu's tasty cousin, would be the next granola. But then I had my Tofurky moment. And now here I stand, having built a company that's so interesting and unusual that some people think there might be money in a book about it.

I love this story. I lived it. It has all the ingredients of great literature—dreams, conflict, suffering, epiphanies, and treehouses. However, the smart money today doesn't care about any of that. It's only looking for a niche in the market where it can quickly build a shiny new brand that lures in armloads of venture capital. The not-quite-as-smart money finds its niche and then builds an attractive top line as quickly as possible so it can sell most or all of its equity to a company like General Mills or Amazon. If that's where you want to go, then this may not be the book you're looking for.

The Tofurky story is the opposite of smart money. It's a story of bootstrapping my way down a path to right livelihood, which sounds kind of quaint, now that I'm typing this. It's a story from olden times, a story about not fitting in with the smart-money and instead building a business that fit me. It's the story of working very hard, living on very little, and diligently striving to become less stupid, mistake by mistake, year after year. It's the story of struggling for twenty years to become an overnight success.

If this *is* the book for you, it's probably because you have a good idea for a business, and you don't have access to armloads of money, ventured or otherwise. You've got something that you're ready to pour your actual *life* into rather than the money that you might otherwise invest, if you had a lot of money, which you don't.

If this is the book for you, then you may also be standing at the trailhead where I stood in 1981. When I stood on that spot, there were no maps or signs, just faint, inviting deer trails leading into the primeval forest of the early natural foods movement. Now here you are, peering into the same dimly lit future. Reasonable people tell you that your idea isn't really worth the risk. You think it might be. They say you don't know enough about business. You agree with that, but you're willing to learn as you go.

I was a lot less reflective in 1981. I just grabbed my daypack and took off, hacking my way through the brush. And things worked out. My little trail became a road to success that I couldn't possibly have mapped out beforehand. It's still taking me into wonderful, new, unmapped territory—like this book—that was never part of the original plan.

That's how I got here, by plunging ahead and learning from my mistakes, and that's the story I'm about to tell you. I'll tell it as faithfully as I can. I'll try to point out the mistakes I made along the way, so you are more likely to avoid them. At the end of each chapter, I'll take a moment to offer a few more pointed lessons about how to go about this business of bootstrapping. Mostly, though, I'll just tell you the story of my happy journey and hope that you take away a few lessons that will help your story to be happy too.

If that sounds like the sort of business book you're looking for, then so be it. I like you already and wish you the best.

Cheers!

2020 Tofurky Logo *(The Tofurky Company)*

HEADWATERS

I n which I am born into a loving and creative family that not only tolerated but nurtured my picky eating and then sent me off to college, where I studied graffiti, became a vegetarian, loaded twenty-eight at-risk kids into a Volkswagen van—thus putting them at greater risk—and landed my first job as a wandering naturalist.

Once your business makes it, the question everyone asks is where your idea came from. I get that all the time with Tofurky, and the answer I usually give is that I noticed how a growing number of vegetarians needed to have something to eat at Thanksgiving, so I created a product to meet that need, and now here we are, five million Tofurkys later. That's more or less what happened, but Tofurky happened in 1995, and by then I had already been selling plant-based protein and losing money for fifteen years.

To really answer where Tofurky came from, we have to go back to the tempeh business I started in December of 1980, Turtle Island Soy Dairy. But before we can get to Turtle Island Soy Dairy, we have to go back another four years to visit the Farm commune in Tennessee and pick up a tempeh starter kit. And before that—

well, there's me, right? I didn't just appear out of nowhere as a fully formed tempeh maker. I started out in a hospital five blocks from the White House on the afternoon of April 20, 1951, as Richard Seth Tibbott.

The businesses we build are usually extensions of who we are more than ideas we have that magically take root. That's why it's so hard for me trace the headwaters of this business back to any particular moment. The headwaters of Tofurky could be any of a half-dozen little streams that went into forming me, my values, and my vision for how life should be.

The Penguins of Washington, D.C.

There was nothing at all in my youth to suggest that I would ever become a vegan, much less an international producer of fine vegan foods. I grew up eating meat—lots of meat and lots of dairy—every day. Having lived through the Great Depression of the 1930s, my parents associated eating meat, cheese, and milk with survival foods. If you had those proteins, you were making it back then. I had a great childhood, but not a vegan one.

As a kid, I was spindly and a picky eater. I didn't care much for meat. My favorite alternative was two slices of Wonder Bread slathered with butter and brown sugar. At dinner, I'd only eat potatoes and Jell-O—hold the fruit, please. I liked the fresh baby peas that Mom sometimes shucked for me and I liked tomato juice, but that was it for vegetables.

In high school, I replaced the brown sugar sandwiches with a daily hamburger at the Little Tavern Burger Shoppe. At dinner, I ate chicken, meatballs, and chopped sirloin steaks. Pancakes and bacon were a favorite, mouth-watering Sunday morning breakfast. In the summer, we ate fresh-caught crabs from our home on the Chesapeake Bay, and Mom invented something we called "hamburger pizza," which we cooked outdoors on a tiny Hibachi.

I wasn't raised to be a vegan, but I *was* raised by wonderful people who taught me to value family and community, to enjoy creativity, to stick with things—and just to have fun. If we're looking for the headwaters of Tofurky, these values are a better place to look than my diet. There wouldn't have been a product called "Tofurky" if I hadn't been raised to go with what made me smile, and I wouldn't have made it through almost twenty years of hand-to-mouth bootstrapping if I hadn't been raised to stick with things and to value the community that eventually formed around and depended on this business.

I picked up a love for fun at an early age from my dad, Lloyd, and his penguin-themed Christmas cards. The little birds were always cracking jokes and getting into trouble. Penguins were Dad's thing, and at a very early age, they were imprinted on me through the hundreds of penguins that were displayed throughout our house. He even used a penguin to announce my birth. I like to say I was raised by penguins, which is halfway true.

Both of my parents fostered a lighthearted sense of play in my brother and me. They encouraged creativity by setting up carnivals for the neighborhood kids and putting together ad hoc theatrical performances on the front stoop. We created a homemade miniature golf course with short sections of drainpipe set vertically around the backyard.

For Halloween and birthday parties, my mom, Betty, sewed costumes for us to wear as part of the celebration. When my beloved Washington Senators tore the heart from my ten-year-old chest by moving to Minneapolis, Mom made Senators baseball uniforms for my brother Bob and me to wear—complete with suitcases bound for Minneapolis. Mom had a way of imagining something that would be fun and then figuring out how to do it.

Family Christmas card with original art by my dad, Lloyd Tibbott. Dad drew and hand painted three hundred of these every year of his married life. *(Lloyd Tibbott)*

I suppose my entrepreneurial tendencies trace back to her practical creativity. I know that my optimism does.

Although he worked for the US Government, Dad was an artist and poet at heart, and had a great sense of humor. Each year, he hand-painted more than three hundred Christmas cards that featured our family interacting with penguins. People begged to get on his Christmas card list. He also had a knack for making up words. One word I remember is "brisking," as in "the palm trees were brisking in the breeze." That's a beautiful word, isn't it?

"How is the language supposed to grow," he asked, "if we don't create new words?" I've always remembered that question.

By the time I was born, Dad was already fifty-six. My mom was thirty-nine. People ask me what it was like to be raised by older parents, but I've never known how to answer that question because they weren't really old. They were young at heart, and they were always playing games with Bob and me. And when we got tired of the games at hand, they invented new ones for us to play.

The old person in our home was Nana, Dad's mother. She was very old when I was born, having been born herself just one month after the Battle of Gettysburg, in 1863. She was a suffragist, devoted to the advancement of women, and also a rather strong-willed artist. She once applied for a job as an illustrator with the US Government. To get the job, she was told to draw a pocket gopher. She drew a perfect pocket gopher but was told it wasn't good enough. She asked to draw it again. They rolled their eyes.

"A woman just can't do this," they told her. "This is a man's work."

She submitted another drawing. It was rejected. She submitted another, and it was rejected too. This went on until finally, after sixty-three drawings, they relented.

"Okay," they told her, "you've proved your point. The job is yours."

But Nana would have none of it.

"I don't want your job," she said. "I just wanted to prove to you that a woman can draw the same or better than a man!"

Nana was way ahead of her time, and she was stubborn.

After marrying my dad, Mom came home ready to set up a house all her own. Nana would have none of that, either. This was her domain, which she had designed and ruled over for a good thirty years. I have never met a kinder or more positive person than my mother. Faced with Nana's determination to keep ruling over the household, Mom graciously deferred to her mother-in-law to create a harmonious home. Mom just plain loved people. She devoted large chunks of her time to charity, and she kept the family together with her good nature, optimism, and ever-present smile.

Mom's father, Seth—for whom I am named—was a lawyer in Minnesota. He had a love for building tiny houses in the woods, which he called "wigwams." He even built a small wigwam in his backyard in Minneapolis. There was a fireplace, a gramophone record player, a bench that also served as a bed, and shelves and shelves of books. He loved Emerson's essays, Thoreau, Lao Tzu, and many others. Each time he read a book, he made notes on every page with different colored pencils—sometimes in four or five different colors. I loved his tiny backyard wigwam and re-member its musty smell to this day. When I built my treehouse, I was proud to bring up a rug from his little house.

I was lucky to have my brother Bob there looking out for me from an early age. He was two years older than me, and he was definitely part of the Tofurky headwaters. For one, we have a long history of business ventures. As kids, we had newspaper routes and built homemade miniature golf courses for our neighbors. He also brought me into our first food business in the summer of 1964. Early in the morning, he got up and caught crabs on the Chesapeake Bay. Then he'd come home at 9:00 or so and tell me to go sell them, which I did. Using my extensive contacts, I was usually sold out by 9:30. That summer, we grossed $64.

More importantly, in 1981, when I was starting out on my own adventure in the food business, I turned to my brother Bob for help with moving into my first real business space. Thankfully, Bob's brotherly love and commitment to family got in the way of his better judgment. He became my early banker for the many years when no real banker would even think about loaning me any money. It was a risk that he was willing to take for the sake of his brother.

Student Vegetarian

If we want to look for the *plant-based* headwaters of Tofurky, the first hint of that stream starts in 1970, when I went away to study elementary education at a quiet Lutheran college in Ohio. I didn't think too much about what I was eating—or the future, for that matter—until halfway through my time at Wittenberg University. But then one night I had dinner with my roommate Tim at his friend Laurel's house.

Laurel was a lithe, blue-eyed art major at Wittenberg. She had a love for Buddhism, organic food, and Gollum, her Labrador protector. Her studio apartment had a futon mattress on the floor, and brightly printed fabric decorated the walls. A small kitchen was cut off from the room by a beaded curtain. We sat cross-legged on the floor in a darkened room lit by candles shoved into wax-splattered Chianti bottles and ate a meal of lentils, rice, and onions that Laurel had found in *Diet for a Small Planet* by Frances Moore Lappé. It was incredible. In her soft, clear voice, Laurel told us about this amazing new book and why we all needed to "live lightly" for the health of our bodies and the planet.

"We don't need to eat meat to be healthy," she said, in that soft voice I can still hear today. "When we eat beans and grains like this directly, we're living lower on the food chain. That frees up resources to feed more people and saves land for wild animals."

This was one of the first clues about my future that I ever stumbled upon. Those gentle words of hers cut right through my less-than-thoughtful ways of thinking and eating. Why *were* we feeding pounds and pounds of grain to animals in order to produce such a small amount of protein? It made no sense. It was bad for me, it was bad for the planet, and it was even worse for the animals I'd been eating.

The world was changing quickly in those days, and I was well aware of the war in Vietnam, the civil rights movement, the environmental movement, and more. But that meal, and especially Laurel's words, brought me into a deeper kind of awareness. This was one of the first times I really saw a clue of where the world was going and recognized it for what it was. I felt it more than I understood it, but it was a clear conviction, nonetheless. Walking home that evening, I felt good, even hopeful. Somewhere within myself, I understood that this was where I wanted to go—that it was where I *would* go. I could just tell.

Soon after that dinner, I took the first step in that direction by becoming a vegetarian. At the time, that was easier said than done. There was almost nothing out there on the health benefits of a vegetarian diet. The most well-known book on nutrition after *Diet for a Small Planet*, was Adelle Davis's *Let's Eat Right to Keep Fit*. Davis was a pioneering nutritionist, very radical for her day, who criticized doctors for their lack of knowledge about nutrition. She recommended a diet high in whole grains, wheat germ, and vegetables, with no heavily processed foods. Although she wasn't a vegetarian, she slammed the American hamburger as dangerous to one's health.

For a long time, I was a lousy vegetarian. Lentils, rice, and onions became *the* meal for me, but I also remember eating whole boxes of Nilla Wafers too. Cheese, peanut butter, and bread were regular parts of my diet, but I stayed away from fruits and vegetables. With no natural food stores or co-ops nearby, I also had to settle for the accidentally vegetarian items in the local grocery store. I wasn't eating meat, which was good, but I also wasn't taking in much nutrition, which was not so good.

Eventually, though, with help from Laurel and others, I began making my own whole grain bread, granola, and yogurt—three items not found in any nearby stores. The decision to head in this direction became a habit, and then the habit became a more informed habit. This way of "living lightly" became an important element of who I was and who I wanted to be. However, it was still a personal understanding about myself and my own way of living. It didn't affect the future I was preparing for at the time— my career as an elementary school teacher.

Elementary School Misfit

Another possible headwater for Tofurky was my attempt to become an elementary school teacher. At about the same time I became a vegetarian, I was also forced to declare a major. I was a junior in 1971. It was time. What I wanted was a recreation degree that would allow me to become a camp director or something like that, a job that did fun, creative things with kids. The closest thing I could find at Wittenberg was elementary education, so that became my major.

A lot of us bootstrapper misfits get into business because we don't fit in anywhere else, and that's how it went with me and elementary education. I couldn't believe how boring those education classes were. So many words, and for so few ideas! To take my mind off those classes, I decided to order off the menu with classes from all over the curriculum—anything that looked fun. One semester, I even convinced a sociology professor to let me take an independent study in graffiti that took me to public bathrooms all across Ohio, which was more interesting in theory than in practice.

A former English professor of mine, Tony Russell, lived in a stately but weary Victorian house with high ceilings, creaky wooden floors, and a small front porch where we watched the world go by. Tony was in his thirties and had a lean, athletic build from his days as a collegiate wrestler. He had a deep baritone voice and a hearty laugh. He'd moved into the house with his wife and four young children, and already he had become a well-respected figure in the neighborhood. At one time, his neighborhood had been *the* neighborhood in Springfield, Ohio, but by now it was the poor, predominantly Appalachian and African American part of town.

Tony was concerned that local kids weren't getting the after-school support they needed from their parents. Many were latch-key kids who hung out on their own for hours until their parents got home from work. Tony decided to offer his basement as a drop-in center, and with ten of my friends, we set up the Tony Russell Free School. He spread the word, and on our first day, the Free School was packed with elementary school kids.

We played games, painted murals, helped with homework, and generally tried to expose these kids to new ways of looking at the world. One day, I brought my '64 Volkswagen van to the school and offered to take kids on a field trip to the biggest park in town. The kids were wild with excitement. They all wanted to go. The van legally seated six people with seat belts, but the kids kept piling in. Who was I to say no? By the time we shut the van doors and began our two-mile creep to the park, we had twenty-eight kids on board.

"Whoa!" said Donny, one of my favorites. "You're gonna bust an axle!"

Upon reflection, I see now that this was a real possibility. Fortunately, the axle held up and everyone had a great time at the park. However, do not attempt this at home. Actually, do not attempt this *anywhere* after 1972.

It was at the Free School that I first became aware of the punishment these kids experienced at the local elementary school. Donny suffered more than most. He was smart, active, and funny, but he came from one of the poorest families on the block. His parents had come to Ohio from Oklahoma, and Donny always wore his trademark felt cowboy hat over his longish hair. One cold day, Donny came to Free School with his hair all wet. It was cold outside, so I asked him why.

"Teacher put my head under the faucet," he said.

"Why did she do that?"

"I missed too many spelling words."

I couldn't believe it.

"Do your parents know about this?"

"Yeah," he said. "They say I have to learn my letters."

We never used punishment of any kind at the Free School, and for us, the kids were always engaged, excited, and—for the most part—well behaved.

The Free School became the best education class I ever took in college. It encouraged me to take ideas and bring them life—my first encounter with entrepreneurship. More than that, it brought home the idea that teaching kids meant taking care of kids—or to put it another way, that taking care of them needs to happen first, before you can teach them.

Good as it was, though, the Free School ruined me for public schools—at least the ones in that town. A year later, I was a student teacher standing in that same elementary school classroom where teachers doused kids' heads with cold water for failed spelling tests and whacked them with rulers. The place was heavy with bad, bad vibes. Nobody wanted to be there, not me and not my students.

I loved kids, and up to that point I'd thought that teaching kids would be a decent career for me, but I just couldn't be in a place like that without the power to change it. In a panic, I went back to my advisor's office and asked him to send me to some other school. Certainly, this couldn't be the whole story of elementary education.

"I'm sorry," he told me.

"I'm sorry too," I told him. "I'm sorry for those kids."

"No," he said. "What I mean is that this is where you've been assigned. I can't make any changes at this point. You'll have to love it or leave it."

I decided to leave it. I walked out of his office and dropped out of school.

Making the decision to drop out of student teaching—and college—was a major step for me. After my decision to become a vegetarian, it was the second time I'd made a major decision based on ethics. As time passed, it became easier to not be involved in things that felt wrong like war, environmentally unsound ways of living, and abusive treatment of animals.

That's one reason why this might be the headwaters for Tofurky. Tofurky was invented for misfits, for all those vegetarians who didn't really fit in at Thanksgiving. It allowed them to be true to themselves and still be there with their cousins and parents. It's an inclusive product, a peacemaker.

Wandering Naturalist

Dropping out of school for the right reasons felt great in the moment, but I had no Plan B. Having no Plan B, as you will see, is a life-long pattern for me. Having things work out in spite of my lack of planning is another pattern that traces back to this same event.

I applied for teaching jobs at a couple of progressive schools. They were polite in their responses, gently pointing out that they couldn't really hire me if I didn't have a degree. Then I remembered the little outdoor education center that was called "Glen Helen" or just "The Glen." Antioch College ran this nature center, which was set in a thousand-acre nature reserve that served as refuge for people and wildlife from the encroaching, monocrop farmlands that surrounded it on all sides.

Walking into the Glen, I was met with cool, fresh air and bird songs echoing throughout the stout beeches, oaks, and maples. A yellow mineral spring bubbled out of the rocks. Ponds were alive with dragonflies and frogs. It was said that before white settlers came to Ohio, the forests were so thick that a squirrel could cross the whole state without touching ground. Standing in the cathedral of pine trees at the Glen, it was easy to imagine.

I was no naturalist, but I was running out of options, so on a cold January day in 1973, I crossed the wooden bridge to the Glen Helen Outdoor Education Center. Big, soft flakes of snow drifted down through the trees. The woods were unusually quiet, but as I walked up to the center, I could hear the shouts and laughter of children. Ah, I thought. That's what I'm talking about.

I walked in and was soon talking to Doug, the camp director, a tall man with a big laugh. He sat me down at his small, cluttered desk and patiently explained how the outdoor program worked. It was staffed by students from Antioch. They were paid three credits, room and board, and twenty-five dollars per week for one semester of work. A new semester had just started, he told me, so they were fully staffed.

"But listen," he said. "Stay for dinner anyway. I can at least feed you."

The dining hall was filled with excited kids. In one corner, a guy my age was surrounded by a group of twelve-year-olds, all of them gushing about the day's discoveries. The room was electric with their excitement as they all talked at once, trying to report everything they'd seen and learned. Before dinner, six other kids gave a detailed weather report—high and low temperature, relative humidity, barometric pressure, and wind speed. Cheers went up with the night's forecast of clear skies for stargazing.

After dinner, the staff and kids migrated over to a small telescope in the middle of a field where Doug pointed out Orion's belt, the big and little dipper, Cassiopeia, and other constellations. I couldn't believe what I was seeing. The whole place stood in such stark contrast to the student teaching gig I'd just dropped out of. This was what I wanted to be a part of. I wanted kids to be excited to learn, to be encouraged and loved. When it was finally time for me to head back to my lonely apartment, I went to Doug and tried to thank him for everything, but I choked up before I could get my thanks out.

Doug laid his great bear paw of a hand on my shoulder.

"I like you, Seth," he said. "I think you have great potential."

He looked me over and smiled.

"I can't afford to pay you anything because our staff is full. However, if you want to be an intern here and train to be a naturalist, I can offer you room and board for the next two months, and then in March, you know, we're starting a new center south of here. I could give you a job there."

I didn't have to think about it.

"Yes!" I told him. "Thank you."

Over the next six months, the natural world opened up for me in ways I'd never dreamed possible. For two months, I interned with the same guy who had listened to the excited kids in the dining hall. He turned me on to the flora and fauna of the Glen— especially birds. How had I not noticed birds all my life? I wanted to go back to every place I had ever lived or visited with my new set of eyes.

Then Doug sent me as a brand-new teacher and naturalist to the new Woodland Altars Outdoor Center in southern Ohio. The camp was made of large stands of deciduous trees and rolling meadows, with a lodge, sleeping huts, and a hundred-year-old log cabin that had been built by early settlers. Every week I got a fresh "trail group" of sixth-graders—five kids from largely white, suburban Dayton and five from largely black, inner city Dayton. It was a great mix. I taught them about the local ecology as we tramped along the camp's trails. On the last day, we hiked five miles over a network of overgrown country roads to a World Heritage site that is thousands of years old, the Great Serpent Mound, which depicts a three-hundred-foot-long serpent swallowing an egg.

That fall, I returned to Wittenberg and finished my degree by student teaching first-graders in a less insane school. They even offered me a full-time job afterwards, and I probably would have taken it too, except that by then I had resolved that the only classroom I wanted to teach in was one without walls and in which I could create with the kids. So two seconds after they handed me my diploma, my roommate Tim and I headed west in his ancient Volkswagen, dubbed the "Buffalo Runner." Inspired by the cover of Joni Mitchell's album *For the Roses*, our destination was Oregon, and that was the entirety of our plan.

We had a great trip west, and I could write a whole book about my next half-decade in Oregon, which was amazing. However, I'm going to summarize. In brief, I found what I was looking for, the classroom without walls, the school that I could help build, by landing a job as a naturalist with suburban Washington County's outdoor school program in the Portland area.

The environmental camp program had been honed over many years. The program ran seven weeks of camps in the fall and seven more in the spring. Each Monday morning, three classes of neatly dressed sixth-graders arrived via school bus and were met by a raucous chorus of welcome songs from the staff of high school volunteers and paid staff. Each Friday afternoon, they left with dirt under the fingernails—often in their hair—and tears in their eyes. I was one of three paid naturalists who trained the high school kids to lead teaching activities with the sixth-graders. More than that, though, we helped the sixth-graders and their

Getting kids excited about insects and spiders as a wandering naturalist in 1975.
(Jim Wells)

high-school leaders to have face-to-face encounters with the natural world.

The naturalists were a mix of retired forest and conservation workers and young, energetic environmental educators fresh out of college. This made for a nice multi-generational vibe. We were piloting a new program called "Sunship Earth." The idea was to give kids memorable experiences that would teach basic ecological concepts. To teach kids the concept of adaptation, for example, we turned the kids into squirrels by taping their thumbs to their hands and then giving them peanuts to eat. It was creative and successful, and the kids loved it. If that wasn't enough, the people I worked with were some of the most positive-minded and talented people I've ever met. They are still among my most cherished friends. The energy at the camp was so positive, I hardly needed to get paid.

But the amazing thing was that I *did* get paid. In retrospect, it wasn't much, but I was living at a camp, so I had free room and board and nowhere to spend money. Between the fall and spring sessions—and then eight-week summer gigs with Jimmy Carter's Youth Conservation Corps for high school students—I was able to support myself by working about six months out of the year. The rest of the year was spent sleeping on couches, living in tipis, and traveling all over in whatever funky, five-hundred-dollar station wagon I was driving at the time. These were fun, creative, low-on-the-food-chain years spent among a loose-knit community that I treasured. It was a great life. I highly recommend it for twenty-somethings—and retired conservationists.

In looking for where Tofurky came from, there are a lot of possible starting places. Wherever the headwaters lie, I know that the Tofurky River flows through these years as a naturalist. This was where I got used to not fitting into conventional systems—or more importantly, to building new and more creative systems where I did fit. That was certainly a necessary skill I needed to start a new business that fit me.

It was also during these years that I discovered the practice of what we called "magic" at outdoor school, a playfulness of imagination that draws people away from what they expect and invites them instead to use their imaginations. I'd seen plenty of magic from my parents as I grew up, of course, so I was ready for it when I arrived at outdoor school. However, as a paid professional, I learned how to create magic of my own and share it with others on a regular basis. Magic would soon become the secret sauce for Turtle Island Soy Dairy and, later, Tofurky itself.

20/20 HINDSIGHT
You Say "Misfit" Like It's a Bad Thing

Growing up as a child raised by penguins, I always felt a little different from the other kids. That made life kind of hard in junior high and high school, where it's all about being one of the cool kids or at least fitting in. The misfits in junior high and high school are the losers, the nerds, the social outcasts.

But that all changed when I went away to college. By the 1970s, the misfits were the cool kids because they didn't fit into the social norms of the day. Suddenly I found myself sitting in a place of honor for not fitting in. I remember one young woman I liked who called me "the upside-down man." She couldn't have given me a higher compliment.

At that point, I started ordering off the menu that had been laid out for me by the social powers that be. I became a vegetarian. I created my own independent study classes and spent long hours teaching myself how to teach at the Tony Russell Free School. These adventures in not fitting in were my first runs at entrepreneurship and probably the best things to come out of those years. They made me look beyond the world as we knew it and peer into the world that might be. They eventually led me to let go entirely of my plans to become a conventional teacher and instead pursue the life of a wandering naturalist, an occupation that is made for misfits.

Patagonia founder Yvon Chouinard says that entrepreneurs are basically juvenile delinquents. They look at how things are and think, "That sucks." Then they do something different that makes more sense. Is that your story, bootstrapper? If so, I hope you find it encouraging. It's amazing how many great new businesses were founded by know-nothings, high-school dropouts, social outcasts, and other misfits.

Misfits may have to work harder to forge their new reality than people with more polished skills for the old reality do, but misfits also have some big-time positives going for them. They aren't satisfied with the status quo, and that helps them see better ways of doing the same old things. They're used to being ignored or even mocked, so they can push ahead with what they envision even when others ignore or make fun of it. They can work without the instant gratification of outward success or approval because they haven't really had much of that from the beginning.

George Bernard Shaw said, "The reasonable man adapts himself to the world; the unreasonable one persists in trying to adapt the world to himself. Therefore, all progress depends on the unreasonable man." That's us—misfits. We're the agents of change around here. So don't let your "misfit-ness" keep you from starting your business. The fact is, it's a prerequisite for entrepreneurship. So get out there and do what you do best by not meeting anyone's expectations but your own.

TEMPEH

I n which I visit with twelve hundred hippies, discover the next granola, amass a huge personal fortune, and disastrously allow a menstruating woman into my tempeh shop. As environmental jobs become endangered at the beginning of the Reagan presidency, and as the elementary education system continues to not be a good fit for me, I follow my prematurely retired naturalist friends into the world of business, to their and my own amazement. Here begins the story of the business that eventually becomes The Tofurky Company.

Potential bootstrappers, almost everything you need to know to run a successful business—even a basic understanding of how to run a successful business—is something you can learn or hire out. But you can't hire someone to enjoy the work for you. If you want to bootstrap a business of your own, make sure that the work itself is something you care about and enjoy. Especially in the early days of your business, bootstrapping consists mostly of just you and the work. Your paycheck is the pleasure you get from that work. Money has little or nothing to do with it.

Former Wandering Naturalist

By the late 1970s, I'd managed to engineer a nice little living for myself by teaching environmental education at outdoor schools and summer youth programs in Oregon. I worked for twenty-five weeks out of the year at $150 a week, plus room and board. Let's not forget the room and board. For the rest of the year, I learned how to stretch my savings. I spent time visiting friends, sleeping on couches in funky rentals, or making a place for myself in tents, tipis, and barns. One of my favorite winter pastimes was hitch-hiking around southern states searching for the fabled ivory-billed woodpecker. I wasn't rich, but I didn't feel poor at all.

As much as I enjoyed the nomadic lifestyle, however, I valued family and community too much to keep sleeping on other people's couches. I wanted a couch of my own, and three hundred dollars a month wasn't going to get me there. And then my friend Bill, another wandering naturalist, redefined what "business" meant by starting his own boot-repair business. That business enabled him to build a cabin on his own land and make a living without having to work a conventional job. It was a form of independence. Because I was basically unemployable *except* as a wandering naturalist, that kind of financial independence was attractive.

However, I doubt I would have done anything with business if two things hadn't happened. First, the most environmentally friendly president since Theodore Roosevelt, Jimmy Carter, somehow lost the election to the least environmentally friendly president up to that time, Ronald Reagan, whose agenda included cutting funding for anything that had the word "environmental" in its title. Second, I found tempeh on not just *a* farm but *the* Farm in Tennessee, and I could tell that tempeh was going to be the next granola.

The Farm

In the summer of 1977, I landed a summer job as a naturalist at a Youth Conservation Corps camp near Greenville, Tennessee. This meant that I could work in the Appalachian Mountains, which I loved, along with other naturalist friends from Oregon. It also meant I'd make an extra thousand dollars over the summer, and that would help pay for some excellent winter travel.

Even better, though, was that I could visit the Farm, a commune south of Nashville. The idea of living communally out in the country had started to take hold in my thinking. This wasn't unusual during those years. Many people were trying to get "back to the land" through communal living. Most communes failed, often catastrophically, but this place had staying power.

I'd learned about the Farm from reading books about the community's founder, Stephen Gaskin. Stephen was an ex-Marine and English professor at San Francisco State whose writing class evolved into an open discussion group that become known as "Monday Night Class." By 1970, his classes were attracting more than a thousand Bay Area hippies every Monday.

Stephen talked about his experiences with psychedelic drugs and lectured on the importance of ecological awareness. His beliefs were an eclectic blend of what he considered the best parts of all of the world's great religions, from Christianity to Zen Buddhism and beyond. He pared down high spiritual concepts to easily understood teachings that resonated deeply with me. This was the age of guru, and Stephen was mine.

In 1970, Stephen cancelled the Monday Night Class to travel across the country for speaking engagements. Many students begged him to let them come along. Stephen agreed but said that everyone had to get their own transportation that they could also live in. On Columbus Day 1971, a caravan of eighty rickety school buses, VW vans, and campers set out to follow Stephen's tour of college campuses and churches. Four months later, these fellow travelers resolved to stay together as a community and head back to Tennessee. In the fall of 1971, they purchased a thousand-acre tract of land for seventy dollars per acre near the town of Summertown, about an hour's drive south of Nashville. The new community was simply named "the Farm." It soon became home to more than a thousand hippies from all over the country.

From the start, the Farm was a generous spiritual community of high ideals and not much money. All the residents took a vow of poverty and owned little more than the clothes on their backs. They tried to be as self-sufficient as possible, which included growing their own food. I was particularly interested in the Farm's diet. I'd been a vegetarian since 1972, but the Farm preached a "pure vegetarian" diet, which meant no eggs, no dairy, and no meat. Today we call this a vegan diet.

"I have been to pig stickings and rice boilings," Stephen said, "and rice boilings have better vibrations than pig stickings." This was the first time I'd heard anyone mention anything about the cruelty associated with eating animals, and he said it five years before the founding of PETA, the first nonprofit to advocate for the ethical treatment of animals.

Feeding the growing population of the Farm was a challenge. With their spiritual mandate to eat no flesh, the Farm turned to growing soybeans. They sent a resident named Alexander Lyon to the National Institute of Health's library in Maryland to find out what products could be made from soybeans. Lyon had a PhD in Microbiology, and he came back with lots of ideas. He discovered ways to make vegan milk, yogurt, cheese, and ice cream years before they were produced commercially in the United States. The Farm never capitalized on any of these innovations, but many of the products you see in stores today can be traced back to this community of hippies in Tennessee.

As influential as Stephen's spiritual teachings were for me, the groundbreaking *The Farm Vegetarian Cookbook,* published in 1975, had just as big of an impact. Louise Hagler wrote that the cookbook was intended to help as many people as possible be vegetarian "without turning them off and making them think that it's strange or weird, and to let people know that it tastes good, looks good, is nice, graceful, that it can be a turn-on, that it'd be really neat to eat, and make you look forward to meal-times, and make you happy to eat such good food."

That made sense to me, so I tried it. Using *The Farm Vegetarian Cookbook* as my guide, I started making several protein-loaded dishes from soybeans. My staples were pressure-cooked soybeans and tortillas or veggie burgers made from soy grits. This helped to calm my mother, who was concerned that I might die from protein deficiency. The dishes were complicated to prepare, but with nothing available in the stores, they became my survival food throughout the mid-1970s.

In the middle of the cookbook, I read about a new, fermented soy food called "tempeh" that people on the Farm were getting excited about. Tempeh is a staple food of Indonesia. It's made by mixing the dried spores of *Rhizopus oligosporus* mold into a batch of lightly cooked, dehulled soybeans. Then you cover the beans and let them sit overnight in a warm place. The mold binds the beans together into a solid white cake that you fry slowly in oil or margarine. Cooked tempeh digests easier than plain boiled soybeans do. The cookbook assured me that tempeh was "easy to make in your home," and invited me to send away for my own tempeh starter and split dehulled soybeans. With no tempeh yet available in stores, the Farm's starter culture became a vital, pioneering source of this unique protein.

Tempeh made environmental sense too. With animal-based protein, you typically use twelve to fifteen pounds of plants to get a single pound of animal protein. With tempeh, you start with a single pound of soybeans and end up with almost two pounds of protein. That means you can harvest much more protein per acre of farmland, and that also means you can feed more people without encroaching on wildlife habitat.

As a diehard fan of all things Stephen, the summer job in Tennessee felt like a pilgrimage to Mecca. It was the perfect opportunity to visit the Farm that I had read so much about. I would also be able to find some of this tempeh and try making it at home. I had no plans for tempeh other than making it for myself and sharing it with friends, but apparently tempeh had plans for me. It was soon to become the starting point for the business I hadn't yet imagined and my north star for the next two decades. Totally oblivious to all of the above, I loaded up the white, 1964 Rambler station wagon that I'd named "Don Quixote" and started off toward the Volunteer State and my summer gig.

On one of the first weekends off, I decided to make the five-hour drive to visit the Farm. Three other comrades decided to go with me. We stopped to ask for directions many times. Invariably, each person asked us the same thing: "Y'all ain't from around here, are ya?" Then they gave us a long list of strange directions like turning left where the old barn used to be or where there's this tree that looks just like a merry-go-round. They'd invariably finish with, "Y'all can't miss it."

We finally found our way to the Farm. In 1977, the Farm had a population of 1,200, all of them hippies, so they outnumbered the residents of nearby Summertown two to one. Given the conservative bent of 1977 southern Tennessee, you might expect to see *some* kind of discontent with the Farm, but then again, the Farm was a paradox of ideas. The residents smoked lots of marijuana, but they abstained from alcohol and tobacco. They didn't have anything to do with organized religion, but they treated the

Ten Commandments reverently as "tripping instructions." They were sexually active, but they believed in marriage.

"If you are having sex," Stephen taught, "then you are engaged. If you're pregnant, then you are married."

In some ways, they fit right in too. They were against synthetic birth control like the pill, and they were against abortion. To provide an alternative to abortions, the Farm midwives offered to deliver any woman's baby for free and, if desired, to place it in a loving home on the Farm, promising to give the baby back to the mother should she change her mind. They could barely support themselves, but they gave food and clothing to local disaster victims after a tornado ravaged Tennessee in 1974.

We pulled into a simple structure called the Gatehouse and found out that we weren't the only ones who thought it would be a good day to visit the Farm. About twenty people sat around in the small front room of the Gatehouse waiting to get the attention of one of the three long-haired men in overalls who ruled the facility.

There was a lot of pressure on the Gatehouse crew to get it right, to keep out any souls that might be a danger to Farm residents, a large proportion of whom were young kids. It took us most of the afternoon, but eventually they agreed that our small party of naturalists was okay. They directed us to a visitors' tent, where we would be fed and housed for one night.

We drove down rutted dirt farm roads through fields of soybeans, corn, and vegetables to a thirty-by-forty-foot canvas tent. In the middle of the tent was a kitchen and eating area, and on the perimeter were smaller sleeping chambers separated by thin, bright sheets of cloth. Several women busily prepared supper, and they assigned us to cornhusking duty. We husked a large pile of Silver Queen corn only to learn that the propane tank had just run out, so there wouldn't be any hot water. Given that the rest of dinner was ready, we sat down to eat our meal of pressure-cooked soybeans, nutritional yeast gravy, and raw sweet corn. We were all amazed at how good the corn tasted without being cooked.

Early the next morning, we woke to a parade of hippies wrapped in tattered blankets heading down to meditation meadow for Sunday services. I was excited to go too, since I'd only heard Stephen teach on a cassette tape. Hundreds of people sat in cross-legged silence on the east-facing hillside in the soft predawn light. Bird calls echoed through the summer woods. A flower-scented breeze blew gently over the worshippers. The silence lasted about twenty minutes and was broken by a hearty one-minute chant of *om* as the sun rose into view.

As the *om* settled, a tall, thin, long-haired man rose up to address the crowd. People leaned slightly forward as Stephen began to speak. He spoke about doing something noble, like saving the world and all sentient beings and the vow of the Bodhisattva. After about thirty minutes, he finished with, "Sometimes when the wind blows, I can feel it blowing through us like we were a field of wheat. I can feel the wind in everybody's hair besides mine, and I know that we're not that different than a field of wheat. The wind blows, and our season passes too, just like the season of wheat passes. We'd better do it while we're ripe, before our season passes."

After Stephen finished, the people headed back to their tents and school buses for breakfast before a day of chores unfolded. My friends and I went back to the visitors' tent and ate an oatmeal breakfast. Then we got ready for the four-hour drive back home. The Farm had treated us to two good meals and a place to sleep, and although it was clear that the Farm needed money—for more propane, for example—their fee for room and board was zero dollars. I was touched by their generosity, and it's been something I've tried to emulate ever since.

They hadn't fed us any of the tempeh that I had hoped to try for myself, but before we left, I wandered down to the Soy Dairy, which was in a wooden, barnlike structure with a large round window on the front, just under the apex. Walking in, I noticed the unmistakable smell of sour soybeans. To my nose, it wasn't a bad smell, but it was still sour. Off to the side, they'd turned a closet into a small incubation chamber. A long-haired man in denim overalls was cleaning up and soaking beans for Monday's tofu batch. He wore an old cloth apron over his overalls, and his hair was neatly tied back into a ponytail.

"Howdy!" I said. "I'm just passing through and wanted to see if I could buy any tempeh or tempeh starter."

"Sorry, man," he said. "Tempeh is a rare treat around here. Whenever we make it, the cakes disappear *fast* from the Farm Store."

I was bummed but also intrigued. Was tempeh really that good?

"Everyone here loves tempeh," he said.

That was a lot of people to like something that much.

"But hang on," he said. "We just started selling tempeh starter. You can order some at The Gatehouse on your way out. It's like three bucks. Then you can make some for yourself."

Whoa! Apparently, I'd found the one place in America where I could get tempeh spores. This was *fantastic*. We stopped at he Gatehouse on our way out. I filled out an order form and handed over three dollars. Those turned out to be the best three dollars I ever spent.

A couple of weeks later, I checked the mail and found a padded envelope from the Farm addressed to me. I took it to my tent—yes, we lived in tents—and poured the contents onto my bunk. The kit consisted of a tiny, two-ounce jar of jet-black liquid and a folded-up, 11x17 inch sheet of paper that explained how to make tempeh. The jar was full of *Rhizopus oligosporus* mold. The instructions were a map for the next twenty years of my life.

The Farm's spiritual leader, Stephen Gaskin, delivering his weekly Sunday morning sermon in the meditation meadow, Summertown, Tennessee. *(The Farm Photo Archives)*

The First Batch of Tempeh

The following weekend, I began my tempeh career by following as best I could the instructions that came with my starter kit from the Farm. They were incredibly detailed, all of them laid out in tiny purple letters. Photos of what good quality tempeh was supposed to look like made my mouth water. I understand that this is not the reaction most people might have to mold, but for me, these moldy rectangles of soybeans looked like high-end filets.

I'd studied the instructions and photos all week and snuck into town to get my supplies. *The Farm Cookbook* claimed that on the

Farm, "children come back for seconds and thirds." It was time to see for myself if tempeh was really that good.

After the enrollees left on Friday, I put a pound of soybeans into a pot of hot water in the kitchen and left them soaking overnight. That was step one. The next morning, the swollen beans had developed a slight vinegary smell. Small patches of foam floated on top of the water. I poured the beans into the sink and rinsed them. Then I began the long, arduous task of dehulling.

Even with the help of my girlfriend, Rhonda, and a few others who pitied me, dehulling a pound of soybeans took a full hour. We each grabbed a handful of beans and rubbed them vigorously between our hands until all the hulls were removed and the beans had split neatly into two halves. Writing that down, it sounds pretty easy, I know, but it really wasn't. Hull-wise, soybeans are surprisingly resilient.

Once the beans were dehulled, I put them into a cooking pot, lit the stove, and heated them to a low rolling boil. A few hulls were mixed in, so I skimmed them off with a little strainer. Then I turned down the heat and left the pot full of soybeans simmering for an hour. Rhonda and the others took off at that point, but I couldn't take my eyes off the soybeans. I just stood there and watched them cook.

When the beans were fully cooked, I spread them out on cookie sheets that I'd lined with dishtowels. The idea was to dry the beans by having the towels soak up the moisture. This proved to be harder than expected in the humid heat of a Tennessee afternoon, but with patience and more dishtowels, I finally got them dry, or at least dry*ish*.

Now came the magic moment. It was time to dig out my little bottle of jet-black *Rhizopus oligosporus* culture and add that to the beans. The bottle really did seem magical too, like something from *Alice in Wonderland*. I put the cooked, dried beans in a ce-

Tempeh

Tempeh is a good tasting, high protein food made from soybeans. Like sourdough bread, miso, sauerkraut, and others, it is made by the natural process of fermentation. For the people of southeast Asia, tempeh has been a staple protein for centuries. In Indonesia, half the annual soybean crop is made into tempeh. Traditionally it is made in villages by putting the beans in large bamboo baskets in a stream. The villagers tramp on the beans with bare feet, while the beans split and the hulls float off downstream. The split, hulled beans are boiled, cooled, and mixed with a piece of tempeh from a previous batch for starter. The beans are then wrapped in broad banana leaves and set in the sun to ferment. After a day or two, the packets are opened and the resulting firm, fragrant white cakes are sold in the marketplace. They can be sliced and sun-dried or fried up immediately and eaten.

Making Tempeh at Home

Making tempeh at home is easy, a lot like making yogurt. All you need for making tempeh is:

Ingredients: soybeans, split and hulled; tempeh starter; and vinegar. (Instructions for whole beans on side two.)

Utensils: a one-gallon cooking pot; a colander; a metal mixing spoon; a small jar; a thermometer; a tempeh container; a slotted spoon.

Tempeh Container: a good tempeh container allows enough air to get in for the tempeh to grow, but without letting in so much that the beans dry out. It also contains the humidity without drowning the mold. A good container could be:

* a frying pan, pot or pie plate with a loose-fitting cover; or
* a dinner plate with a pot lid or inverted pie plate over it; or
* a 9" x 9" covered casserole dish;
* a colander with a lid on it; or
* a cake pan, pie plate, flat bottomed bowl, or pot. Stretch a piece of wax paper, plastic wrap, or tinfoil over the top of the container and tape it down on the sides to hold it in place. The cover should be ¼" or more above the surface of the beans. Punch holes in cover every inch with a nail.

Incubator: where you keep the tempeh container to maintain a stable temperature near 90° while the tempeh does its thing. Some ideas for incubators are:

* a picnic cooler with a small (ornament size or 7½-watt) light bulb wired inside; or
* a closet with a drop light (check temperature occasionally), or
* a shelf above or beside your hot water heater (temperature may vary with amount of hot water being used so check temperature when heater is on pilot and again when heater is on full); or
* an oven with a pilot (check temperature first); or
* in a warm place where heat collects; in a sunny window, in the rafters over a wood stove; or an attic.

FIVE DOLLAR INCUBATOR

Switch

Hole In Lid To Fit Socket
Cut With Sharp Knife

Socket (Rubber or Plastic Insulated)
Fasten To Lid With White Glue

7½-watt bulb

Foam Plastic Cooler

Plug

HOMEMADE TEMPEH

2½ cups (1 lb.) split, hulled soybeans, washed and drained
1 Tablespoon vinegar
1 teaspoon tempeh starter liquid
Makes about 2 pounds of tempeh (12 pieces 4" x 3" x ½")

1. Boiling
Put split, hulled soybeans in cooking pot with 2 quarts water. Bring to a boil and cook at a bubbling boil for 45 minutes.

2. Draining and Cooling
Pour cooked beans into a colander, cover, and let drain and cool for 20 minutes.

3. Making the Starter Liquid
Rinse the packet of dried tempeh starter out well with 3 teaspoons clean cool water. Pour into a small jar, cap tightly, and shake well.

4. Adding the Starter
Put the drained, cooled beans in the well-drained cooking pot. Add 1 Tbsp. vinegar and mix well. Check the temperature down in the center of the beans where it will be warmest—it should be below body temperature or it could harm the starter. If necessary, stir the beans to cool them down. Shake the starter liquid well, add 1 tsp to cooled beans, and mix thoroughly, about a minute. Refrigerate remaining starter liquid. It will keep for 3 weeks refrigerated. Save for the next batch.

5. Packaging the Beans
Make a smooth, lightly packed layer of beans not more than ½" deep in one or more of the tempeh containers, and cover.

6. Growing the Tempeh
Place tempeh containers in the incubator. The temperature should be between 85° and 95°F. —88° is best. This is because temperatures much outside this range can inhibit the tempeh mold and promote the growth of unwanted bacteria that will spoil the tempeh. This is important in the first 12 hours when the tempeh mold gets started. So check the temperature with a thermometer occasionally to make sure the tempeh isn't getting too hot or too cold. Don't incubate in a small airtight box as the mold requires oxygen.

After 12-15 hours at these temperatures, condensation should start forming on the inside of the tempeh container(s). The white mold will begin to show faintly, and it will gradually thicken over the next 3-4 hours. The tempeh is now producing heat, so watch the temperature and adjust as needed. In 19-22 hours the mold will lengthen and thicken luxuriously. At 24-30 hours, it looks like white icing on a cake.

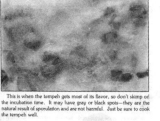

This is when the tempeh gets most of its flavor, so don't skimp on the incubation time. It may have gray or black spots—they are the natural result of sporulation and are not harmful. Just be sure to cook the tempeh well.

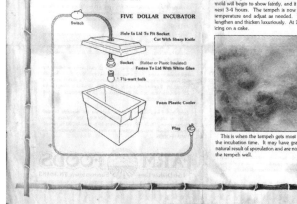

Tempeh making instructions that I received from the Farm with my first order of tempeh starter in 1977. Yes, I am a pack rat. *(The Farm, Summertown, TN)*

ramic bowl, poured the black spores all around the white soybeans, and mixed it all thoroughly.

The last step for Saturday was to dump the mixture of beans and spores into a stainless-steel baking pan that was about half an inch deep. I covered the pan with aluminum foil and poked a hundred little holes in it with a thumbtack. And because Tennessee in summer is itself basically one giant tempeh incubator, all I had to do was put the covered pan on a chair out in the field and wait. They would ferment for twenty-four hours, and then they'd be tempeh.

Late on Sunday afternoon, I walked to the chair with the fermenting soybeans and gently lifted one corner of the foil cover. It smelled great—I can still smell it, in fact—a pleasant, fresh, mushroomy aroma. That made me smile, and I lifted up the rest of the foil. There, covering the entire pan of beans was a thick white carpet of tempeh mold. The mold was so firm that beads of water had formed on it. It looked just like the pictures in the instructions from the Farm. It looked perfect! I hustled the tempeh back to the cook tent where the rest of the staff was sitting around drinking beers.

"Let's cook this up!" I yelled.

Our cook, Debbie, cut the tempeh into three-inch squares and sautéed them perfectly to a golden brown. We added thick slices of fresh tomatoes, Silver Queen sweet corn, and fried okra. What followed was a dinner to remember, a truly magical feast. I've made thousands and thousands of batches of tempeh since that first batch on the banks of the Nolichucky River, but nothing has come close. I can still taste it.

For the other staff members, it was more of a dare to eat moldy soybeans. I found out later that a few actually feared for their lives, this being my first batch of mold and all. Thanks to all that cold beer, however, caution was weakened, and good sense was even weaker. Rhonda later told me that she decided that if she was going to die from eating soybean mold, at least it would be among friends. Those who tried my first batch of tempeh, though, were soon impressed by the tempeh's firm texture and rich flavor, which of course "tasted like chicken." No lives were lost.

I was totally hooked. This was the best plant-based protein I'd ever eaten. Unlike the challenging option of soygrit burgers, which tasted bad and digested worse, tempeh had a pleasing, fully cooked texture about it that felt good in my body. Later I learned that it's the fermentation process that makes tempeh so easy for

The YCC staff sits around the cook tent in Kinser Park, Tennessee, waiting to die after eating my first tempeh batch, incubated earlier that day in a nearby field.
(*Rhonda Frick-Wright*)

the body to assimilate, but that Sunday I just felt good after eating it. I could tell even from this first meal that tempeh was going to be a regular part of my diet moving forward.

The New Granola

When the summer of tempeh finally ended, Rhonda and I loaded up Don Quixote and headed back for another fall session of outdoor school camps. Our first stop was the Florida Everglades. Our second stop was Mt. Katahdin in Maine. Then we decided to actually travel in a westerly direction toward Oregon. One stop along the way was Springfield, Ohio, where I'd attended college, and it was here that the universe gave me a second clue about the future.

Six years earlier, while I was still a student, I'd taken a part-time job at the one and only head shop in that quiet little town. It was exactly what you envision when you read the term "head shop," a dark little underground establishment sandwiched in between two second-hand stores. In addition to the usual smoking apparatus, this was the sort of place where you could pick up affordable blacklight posters, R. Crumb comics, peace buttons, anti-war books, copies of *Mother Earth News*, and whatever else you might need to get stoked for the next big protest.

In this head shop, we sold rainbow-themed bags of something called "granola." You may have heard of it. In 1971, this was the only place in Springfield where you could buy granola. You could make it at home, of course, and many new vegetarians did just that, but at the head shop, it came already mixed, baked, and ready to eat right out of the bag. It was a good seller too, a brilliant cross-marketing initiative for customers who would soon be hungry.

"All right," our customers said. "I'll take a pipe, a pack of Zig-Zags, and, what the hell, give me a bag of granola too."

That wasn't my clue from the universe, however. My clue came on the trip back to Oregon from Tennessee. We drove past the head shop and saw that it had gone out of business. Then we stopped at the IGA grocery store and discovered that granola had escaped from the head shop and taken over the better part of an aisle. There were twenty different brands of granola begging to be bought.

"Whoa," I said. "The hippies were right about granola."

That's when it hit me. If the hippies had been right about granola, what else were they right about? I thought about those twelve hundred hippies on the Farm who had fallen in love with tempeh. I was *sure* they were right. In another six years, I predicted to myself, tempeh would have its own little section at the IGA. I could see it in my mind. I could feel it in my gut. Whoever got ahead in the tempeh game, I thought, was going to make a lot of money.

I didn't do anything with this clue at the moment. I just got back in Don Quixote and drove across the Great Plains. However, I kept that clue about the future tucked away in my brain. I pondered it. I knew that the universe had let me look around the corner at something that was coming our way, and I didn't take it lightly.

Leaving Environmental Education

I stayed with the nomadic lifestyle of the wandering naturalist through 1978 and into 1979, but it was starting to lose some of its appeal. The twenty-eight-year-old isn't quite as free-spirited as the twenty-two-year-old, and at twenty-nine, you look up into the rearview mirror and realize that holy crap—there's a rearview mirror! Existential nausea began to brew within me, and because this was my first experience with existential nausea since that one

Working as a starving naturalist in 1979 near Forest Grove, Oregon, before becoming a starving tempeh maker. *(Jan Muir)*

day of student teaching at the punishment-crazy elementary school, it really got under my skin.

In the winter of 1979, I finished up what I thought was going to be my last federally funded gig as a naturalist in the Portland public schools and moved out to a small retreat center in the foothills of the Oregon Coast Range. The Cherry Grove Center consisted of 160 acres of rolling farmland, a historic log hunting lodge with rooms that were rented out to retreat groups, and a remodeled barn that was home to my friends Garry and Belinda and their two-year-old daughter, Molly, who had been born on the Farm, the first kid in my universe of friends.

We had a dream of starting our own camp and environmental education program at the retreat center. Environmental education was what we knew, so that made sense. The only problem was that someone still had to pay us to do that environmental education, and the money was getting harder to find. Federal funding had all but dried up for programs like the Youth Conservation Corps, and with Oregon starting to head into a recession, there wasn't much state funding available, either. We got by for a while, but we didn't make much money. In 1979, my taxable income was twenty-two dollars.

That's not a misprint.

To supplement that impressively nonmaterialistic income, I started to look again at tempeh as a way to make some money. A lot of retreat groups came to the center on weekends, and Linda, the center's cook, was open to the idea of serving them tempeh as a cutting-edge form of protein. To increase the amount of tempeh I could produce with my picnic-cooler incubator, I lined an abandoned refrigerator with Christmas lights and hooked them up to a poultry thermostat. It worked great, and it allowed me to produce up to ten pounds of tempeh at a time. Linda coated the tempeh with breadcrumbs and baked it for her guests.

Tempeh was still mostly a hobby, but now it provided a little trickle of income. An even bigger pleasure was seeing strangers enjoy my tempeh. It's one thing when it's your friends who tell you how good it is. They could always be saying that to spare your feelings. Strangers don't have that concern. If they like it, it's because it's good stuff, and I was proud of that.

After more than a year of struggling to survive as private environmental educators, Garry and I took jobs at one final, federally funded environmental program. At the last minute, in spring of 1980, the Carter administration came through with money for one more year of the Youth Conservation Corps. We signed on with some other friends to help run a YCC camp on the Kenai Peninsula in Alaska.

We went up in June and came back in October with our minds completely blown by the sheer beauty and magnitude of wilderness there. Garry came back with such a love for Alaska that he spent much of the next three decades living there. I came back loving Alaska too, but by working around the clock all summer and having nowhere to go and nothing to buy, I also came back with $7,500—a fortune—340 times my adjusted annual income for 1979. That huge wad of cash allowed me—or maybe forced me—to step back and ask myself, "Now what, Seth?"

I had no idea, so I ignored the question and moved into a house in Manning, Oregon, with my new girlfriend, Kim. To make money, I did some student teaching in nearby Forest Grove. Subbing forced me to think more seriously about that question of what came next. I didn't want the future to be one in which I lived off of substitute teaching—or even full-time work in a conventional classroom. I didn't fit into that system, and the system wasn't interested in me making changes to it so that I did fit.

I also wasn't ready to give up my six-months-on/six-months-off lifestyle. I liked having the freedom to travel. I liked hanging out with friends for weeks at a time. I liked having the freedom to change course when I got tired of something, or when something got tired of me. That's why the conventional options available to me were so unappealing. That's also why, for the first time, to own amazement, I started to think about venturing into the world of business.

Entering the World of Business

Stephen said, "You can learn to take care of yourself. And that's revolutionary because if you want any independence, it comes with taking care of yourself." I certainly felt the need for that.

"Learn to make a living for yourself and some other people," he also said. "Get strong enough to take care of somebody besides yourself. Don't get caught doing something dumb. Don't get caught in a job that will be phased out when the money gets tough." That all made sense too. I just needed to find the right path toward that independence, a path that didn't include subbing at elementary schools.

My friend Bill was the one who got me thinking about getting into business. In November, just after Ronald Reagan somehow managed to get himself elected, Bill said, "It looks like we've come to the end of the environmental education government gravy train."

"Yeah," I said. And it wasn't just Reagan. It was all of it.

"But," said Bill. "These guys sure do like business, right? So maybe it's a good time to check out that path."

This made perfect sense to me, which made me feel uncomfortable. All the way through college I had ridiculed the business majors, filling my schedule with the more valuable humanities and elementary education courses that I knew would lead to great jobs. Business to me meant Dow Chemical and General Electric and all the other corporations I'd protested during the Vietnam War years. My goal was to do the *opposite* of business, which I had more or less achieved by becoming a wandering naturalist.

Bill had a point about checking out the business path, though. He had just started his own small, boot repair business called Mountain Soles. To learn the business, Bill had already interned with a small shoe repair shop in Portland. Now he was planning to take his business to the parcel of land he just bought in sleepy Trout Lake, Washington. He was going to settle in, build up his business to live on, and build a house to live in. It sounded great to me.

I came up with four possible businesses for myself:

Clock repair. This was inspired by Bill's shoe repair shop, but I didn't actually know anything about clocks or how to repair them.

Writer. I liked to write. I had gotten good grades on papers. My mother liked what I wrote. Yeah, probably not that.

Farmer. I had once fallen off a tractor and nearly killed myself. This one shouldn't even have made the list.

Tempeh maker. It *was* a super food. It tasted better than tofu. I not only knew how to make it, I *enjoyed* making it. And let's be serious—can 1,200 hippies all be wrong?

To seal the deal, the universe sent me another clue. It sat two hundred yards from the little farmhouse Kim and I were renting in tiny Manning, Oregon, and it was called the Java Restaurant. It was probably the only Indonesian restaurant in Oregon at the time. The place was humble but clean, featuring red Naugahyde booths from the previous cafe that had occupied the space, and some cheap batiks and shadow puppets hung on the walls. On our first visit, a lone trucker worked on a hamburger at one side of the restaurant, and a family of tired tourists snipped at one another on the other side. Kim and I took a booth in the middle.

"Selamat sore!" said the owner, Ina, a slender woman with jet-black hair who was probably in her fifties. "That means 'good afternoon' in Indonesian. Can I get you anything to drink or eat?"

"Thanks," I said. "I noticed that you don't have any tempeh on the menu."

"Tempeh!" she barked. "How do you know about tempeh? I have tahu—tofu—but no place where I shop can I ever find tempeh."

"I've been making tempeh for several years now," I said. "I used to make it for a retreat center not far from here. I could try and make some for you, if you want."

"You know how to make tempeh?" she said, eying me more closely.

Tofu was everywhere in Asia, but tempeh was only popular in Indonesia, where it was first produced. Ina's disbelief that a tempeh maker was living in Manning was matched only by my own disbelief that the only tempeh maker I knew about, me, was living practically next door to the only restaurant in Oregon that knew what tempeh was.

Ina ordered two pounds of tempeh on the spot.

"The tempeh has to be good quality or I won't buy it!" she said. "But if it is good, I have many friends who are hungry for tempeh and will buy more."

I went back home and started a two-pound batch of tempeh in the old farmhouse. Old black and white logger photos covered one wall of the kitchen. Those burly loggers in their suspenders and wool shirts had never seen the likes of me packing my cooked, dried, inoculated beans in a small beer cooler with a 7.5-watt lightbulb for heat. I'd done this so many times over the past few years that I was confident of the outcome. The loggers were skeptical.

That night, as Kim and I took a bath together, I laid out my dream.

"I've been thinking of starting a tempeh company, Kim. I think Ina is some kind of sign from the universe that now is the time to start. But I don't know what to call it."

"It has to be catchy," she said. "Magical."

"Yeah," I said. "How about Small Planet Soyfoods?"

"No," she said. "That's okay, but it's plain. Tempeh is new here, so you need something more than just okay."

We thought about it. The water was starting to get not quite warm enough.

"Wait!" she said. "That Gary Snyder book—*Turtle Island*." The idea behind the title is a Native American story where all of North America rides on the back of the giant turtle that's swimming through the ocean.

"Okay," I said.

"We live on Turtle Island," she said, splashing me. "Turtle Island Tempeh!"

That was the perfect name. All I had to do now was make the tempeh to match it.

The next morning, I tiptoed down the stairs to the kitchen. It always felt a little like Christmas morning when I got up to check on a new batch of tempeh. I cracked the lid of the picnic cooler, and there was a beautiful, snowy white bed of tempeh. The familiar, earthy, mushroomy smell permeated the cooler and spread into the kitchen. I wrapped these cakes of what looked to me like perfect tempeh in brown paper bags and headed down the road to the Java Restaurant.

When Ina saw me, she rushed over. I pulled out the tempeh.

"You make this?" Ina asked. "You make this in your house?"

"I did."

"I can't believe you make such beautiful tempeh! I will take ten more pounds."

"Great!" I said. "I'll have it for you tomorrow."

Then Ina turned serious.

"One more important thing," she said, stepping closer to me. "You must never, *ever*, let a menstruating woman into your tempeh shop. It will ruin that day's tempeh, and you will never be able to make tempeh in that shop again!"

"Okay," I said. "I'll remember that."

That afternoon, me and the coincidentally menstruating Kim set up a giant batch of tempeh for Ina. We spread the cooked beans out over the kitchen table and used an electric fan to cool the beans down before putting them into *two* warmed coolers.

When I came down the next morning, I caught a whiff of something all the way up the stairs, and it was something nasty too. It smelled something like soiled diapers.

"Kim!" I called. "Could you come here?"

She came down the stairs, holding her nose.

"What is that?" she asked.

I opened the lids of the coolers, and the smell rushed out and overwhelmed us both. Instead of beautiful white Christmas tempeh ready for Ina, the coolers were filled with slimy brown piles of foul-smelling mush.

We looked at each other in disbelief. And then we laughed.

Millions of soybeans have flowed through my life since that morning in Manning, and menstruating women have made many thousands of perfect batches in my tempeh shops. On that morning, though, tempeh took its rightful place somewhere in the realm between science and magic. I didn't feel at all discouraged. I just started cleaning out those coolers to try again. The age of tempeh had arrived. I could feel a path forming under my feet.

Two weeks later, on December 1, I filed paperwork with the State of Oregon and became the sole proprietor of Turtle Island Soy Dairy.

"Let the wild rumpus begin!" said Kim, quoting her favorite line from *Where the Wild Things Are*.

20/20 HINDSIGHT:
Invest Yourself in a Worthy Mission

Let's wrap this chapter up with a final word about mission. My first glimpse of business as a force for good came from that hippie spiritual commune in Tennessee, the Farm. The Farm had several businesses going on. It produced vegan food, ran a publishing house that was the leading source of vegan cookbooks, and, of course, sold tempeh starter.

These were all business ventures that shared a clear, worthy mission of living in better harmony with the world and improving the lives of others. They needed money from these enterprises, but the money wasn't to create wealth for themselves but instead to push forward their larger vision for how the world should be. They wanted most of all to bring good into the world. That mission also turned them into great models for *how* to run a business that brings good into to the world. They were genuinely kind and generous. The Farm was instrumental in helping me frame my missions in business *and* in life.

Not all businesses have a mission beyond supporting the operators, which is a noble enough mission on its own, but having a mission that goes beyond supporting yourself can be a huge positive for your business. My mission was bringing vegan, low-on-the-food-chain protein to the world. Yours could be any kind of change that you want to see in the world.

You hear people say that what they love about business is business, that they would be happy selling *anything*. I know some people who actually dislike the product they're selling but have still built a business around it. I guess that's fine too, but I think that businesses with larger missions in their hearts are more likely to succeed as bootstraps and more rewarding to build in the long run. In all my years of getting to know other businesses that share the vegan mission, I've never met a single founder who was only interested in making money.

My mission kept me going through a lot of lean years. As you'll soon see, I would never have lasted through the first decade if tempeh had just been my savvy play for big money or me doing business for the pleasure of doing business—because there was no money for a long time, and the pleasure of doing business was pretty painful. The mission was always there as a reward, even when the money wasn't. Tofurky would never have been born if this was just about money.

A worthy mission can keep you going too. It might be the difference between failure and getting to your breakthrough moment. But even if the bootstraps break and things fall apart, which happens, at least you'll have invested yourself into something that was worth doing, something to be proud of, something that made the world just a little bit better.

SOLE PROPRIETOR

I n which I read two chapters of Small Time Operator *four times, spend my $2,500 annual budget in three months, raise the wrong hand at a Small Business Administration seminar, and land my first distributor on April Fools' Day. Turtle Island magically changes from an idea dreamed up in a bathtub to a real, and sometimes surreal, business for me and my fellow pie-in-the-sky dreamers.*

Bootstrappers, I have yet to meet anyone less prepared for business than I was when I became the sole proprietor of Turtle Island Soy Dairy. One of the benefits of being ignorant, however, is that you don't really know how ignorant you are. You don't really care. And I say good for you. Go do the impossible. Do this thing that makes your loved ones worry about you, and have fun doing it. Even if your business fails, you'll always treasure the buzz and adrenaline of these first, golden, ignorant days.

Bootstrapping

To get this business going, I started with $2,500 of my federally funded Alaska money. (Thank you, Jimmy Carter.) According to my precise calculations, that investment would get me through the first year, and by then I assumed I'd have "positive cash flow," which was a term I'd heard used in conversation, a term that seemed to signify an important turning point in the growth of a business.

There was no Plan B. With Reagan in the White House, federal funding for environmental *anything* was dead, so I was no longer a wandering naturalist. I'd been making a few dollars with substitute teaching through the fall, but as much as I liked the kids, there still wasn't a future for me inside a walled classroom. That hadn't changed since college. As far as I could see, there was no *need* for a Plan B, either. This was going to work because the universe seemed to be behind it and because I was doing something I enjoyed, something that would make the world a little better. I didn't see how it could *not* work, right?

I had three goals for my new business:

1. Create a right livelihood for myself that would eventually pay me a salary of $1,000 a month. That was four times what I'd been living on for most of my career as a wandering naturalist. I couldn't even imagine how I would spend all that money, aside from buying a couch of my own to sleep on.
2. Help to make tempeh the next granola. Here was a sustainable protein that was low on the food chain and that tasted great—how could it miss?
3. Make enough profit to help support a camp or outdoor school and other environmental initiatives. This was a

stretch, I knew, but I thought it would be cool to use my business to support what I then thought of as the opposite of business—community and the environment.

My plan, if you would like to call it a plan, was to keep doing what I'd been doing for the last couple of years—make tempeh. I'd just make more of it. I'd start small by selling tempeh around Portland and see how things went. Probably things would go great because at that time only one brand of tempeh had made its way from Seattle to the shelves of Portland's new natural foods market. The Seattle tempeh wasn't bad, but it also wasn't half as good as Turtle Island tempeh was.

I pitched my plan to the managers of the Hope Neighborhood Food Co-op in Forest Grove, Oregon. The co-op was the local hub for alternative types like myself and one of about a dozen natural food stores in the greater Portland area. It was housed in a renovated creamery building with sturdy concrete floors and walls. In the back corner, next to a fenced-in play area, they had a small café kitchen with sinks, an electric stove, and a second-hand refrigerator. A back door led to a dimly lit warehouse area. Being idealistic and compassionate people, the co-op managers agreed to rent me space in the small café. The rent was twenty-five dollars per month, and the café space was all mine from four in the afternoon, when the café closed, to seven in the morning, when it opened back up.

It was a great deal for a man with a $2,500 annual budget, but an even better deal was all the business coaching that the co-op managers offered me for free. One manager in particular, Robert, knew the natural foods business inside and out. He was a wise man, and he tried his best to counsel me in the ways of margins, mark-up, and pricing. His counsel didn't really take, though. It didn't make a lot of sense to me yet, and it didn't really fit who I was. I was a creative soul, not a numbers guy. My focus was on the tempeh. The business, I assumed, would take care of itself.

When I told my shoe-repairing friend Bill about my new business, he nodded thoughtfully and said nothing for a minute. Then he picked up his well-worn copy of *Small Time Operator* by Bernard Kamoroff and handed it to me.

"This is the Bible," Bill said. "This tells you everything you need to know."

"Thanks," I said. "I'll look it over."

"Everything," he said.

The exterior of the Hope Neighborhood Food Co-Op, circa 1981. *(Robert Grott)*

I tried to read the Kamoroff Bible. I really did. I made it through about eight chapters, but unfortunately, those eight chapters consisted of stumbling through the first two chapters on four different occasions. It just didn't make sense. Or maybe it did make sense, but it didn't make as much sense as playing the mandolin out on the porch or throwing some Frisbee golf with my friends. Kamoroff was writing to business people. I was a tempeh person. I had to be true to myself.

After I'd secured my space at the Hope Co-op, I decided that it was time to stop substitute teaching and concentrate on tempeh full-time. About a week before Christmas break, I told everyone in the teachers' lounge that this would be my last day of subbing.

Nobody said anything.

"I'm going to start a soy dairy right here in Forest Grove," I told them.

Again, there was quiet appreciation of this information.

"I'm going to sell tempeh for a living," I told them, happy and excited.

The quiet began to feel a little uneasy, which made me laugh because of course they wouldn't know what tempeh is.

"It's an Indonesian dish," I said. "It's made from fermented soybeans."

It was still unusually quiet in the teachers' lounge. Most of my colleagues turned back to their lunches. Finally, the fifth-grade teacher smiled at me.

"Well, Seth," she said. "You'll find out quickly whether this is a good idea or not."

It *was* a good idea. Obviously.

"And then," she said, "you'll be able to fall back on teaching."

A sliver of insight from her response might have pierced my thinking at that moment. I remember having to shake off the negative energy in the room, to not let it get into my headspace,

51

so I suppose it *was* in my headspace, at some level. In the end, though, I just couldn't see how something that was obviously so right for me could in any way be a bad idea, even if technically it was a bad idea—on the surface.

A week later, with the business just getting off the ground that December, I decided to take a couple of weeks off for a holiday trip to spend some time with family in Minnesota. I was excited to tell them about my new career and how all the pieces were coming together with my space at the co-op, the Java Restaurant, and the growing natural foods market.

My Aunt Rosie listened dutifully to her young nephew for almost an hour on one of those evenings. Then she fixed her eye on me until I really had no option but to stop talking.

"Seth," she said. "Selling soybean food to the American public is a bad idea."

I wanted to have something to say to that. I wanted to be able to offer her a thoughtful, businesslike counterargument. I wanted to explain how it was a good idea but without relying on the evidence of twelve hundred hippies, granola, menstruating women, or clues from a benevolent universe.

"You might be right," I told her.

"Of course I'm right."

I got up to get us both another piece of her amazing apple pie.

"No one wants to eat soybeans," she said, "and especially not moldy ones."

"Well," I said, smiling at my shoes. I wasn't going to let her negative energy take root.

"Seth," she said. "*Seth*. Look at me."

I looked at her.

"Honey," she said, with all the gentleness she might have used on a five-year-old who had skinned his knee, "this is a meat-eating country, and it will always be a meat-eating country."

Early Equipment

I got back to Forest Grove in January, the month of new resolutions. My business was a month old, and outside of securing space at Hope Co-op and reading two chapters of *Small Time Operator* four times, I had done no business in that month. I finally saw that for this business to take off, I would have to learn how to do business.

This was no warning from the universe, either. This was just me finally looking at what had been so very obvious to Robert, Bill, my associates in the teachers' lounge, and Aunt Rosie. Turtle Island wouldn't make it through many more months like December. I had to get moving. I had to make this thing real. Now all I had to do was figure out what that meant.

I was pretty sure that one thing I needed to do was get better equipment so that I could produce bigger batches of tempeh. Picnic coolers wouldn't handle the volume. The problem, though, was that in 1981 I was one of only a half-dozen commercial tempeh shops in the nation. I couldn't just look for tempeh equipment in the Yellow Pages, which were still yellow in those days, and still pages too. I had to invent it for myself.

I started with an easy target, a new delivery van. By "delivery van," I meant a gray $350 Datsun station wagon that was advertised as having "some body damage." When I went to check it out, I saw that the body damage was the result of having been T-boned by something large and fast moving. The entire driver's side had been pushed back half a foot. The driver's side door was gone entirely. Its bright green replacement was lying in the back of the wagon.

Still, the engine sounded good, and the tires had plenty of rubber, so I paid the man and drove it home happily, with nothing between me and the pavement rolling along on my left, except a

53

seatbelt that wouldn't retract. It was a Saturday, and that afternoon, after a few beers, my friends and I went to work. We held a carjack and a long 4x4 sideways against the left side of the Datsun and jacked it back into place, for the most part. After mounting the door and latching it shut with a small bungee cord, my business van was ready to roll.

The next purchases came together quickly:

- two fifteen-gallon stainless steel cook pots with lids, $120
- one Corona mill for splitting beans, $30
- a used electric motor and miscellaneous pulleys and belts for mixing beans, $16.50
- two large polyethylene mixing tubs, $45
- a used Formica-topped kitchen table, $5
- a large strainer for skimming off hulls of split beans during cooking, $8
- a 115-volt Bock centrifuge for drying beans, $650
- custom food-drying racks, $240
- a used commercial freezer, $300

The last piece of equipment, the incubator in which the mold spores did their magic with the soybeans, was the most important. Remembering the junky old refrigerator that I'd used at Cherry Grove Center, I started looking for a bigger junky old refrigerator that would incubate larger batches of tempeh. So I started looking in old refrigerator junkyards, which are a thing. After a week of searching, I finally found my incubator under the Hawthorne Bridge in Southeast Portland, which in that pre-hipster era was a gritty neighborhood marked by warehouses, junkyards, and large men with death-themed tattoos.

My future incubator was a beautiful, four-door commercial refrigerator with tight-fitting doors and no compressor or cooling coils to get in the way. A hundred dollars later, she was mine. I went right back to Forest Gove and rented a pick-up truck to bring her home, but by the time I got back to the refrigerator junkyard, it was starting to get dark and there was nobody around to help me hoist it into the truck. It was a big unit, so hoisting it into the truck was no small task.

Just down the block, though, was the venerable Produce Row Bar and Grill. I went inside and surveyed the crowd. These were people who hoisted large things for a living. I walked up to a table where four large hoisters of things sat arguing about something to do with diesel mechanics. When they noticed my skinny, vegetarian self standing there, they left off their discussion to consider the anomaly before them.

"I have a great offer for you," I said.

They waited.

"You spend two minutes helping me lift a refrigerator into my truck, and I'll buy you two pitchers of beer. How does that sound?"

Five minutes later, they were no doubt toasting my skinny vegetarian self, and I was on my way to Forest Grove with the last piece of my first commercial tempeh shop. I hadn't made a single batch of tempeh, but at least now I could start making test batches and work my way up toward my dream goal of making a hundred pounds of tempeh at a time.

Early Concerns

By the end of January, things were looking up for Turtle Island Soy Dairy. Things for me, however, were starting to get just a little worrisome. Money, for example, was starting to worry me. The $2,500 that I'd budgeted to get things started was mostly gone now, thanks to the things I hadn't budgeted for. Equipment costs came in higher than planned, and so did packaging, insurance, and taxes. I'd budgeted zero dollars for marketing, and sales expenses were left out entirely, which certainly made sense to someone who was running out of money.

I was also increasingly concerned about my lack of food processing knowledge. It was one thing to make tempeh in small batches for home use. It was another thing to scale the recipe up to a hundred pounds and make the whole batch in a single, eight-hour shift. I came into Hope Co-op every afternoon and carefully prepared the beans, carefully mixed the tempeh and starter, and carefully set up my incubator for the overnight transformation of beans into tempeh. It felt so right each time I did it. The next afternoon, however, I'd return to find a foul-smelling mess in the incubator.

What was I doing wrong? It didn't make sense. I cleaned out each mess and bagged them up as compost for the garden, and then I tried again to do everything just right. I was becoming a hero to the local rufous-sided towhees who liked to dig up the composted tempeh in the garden plot, but to the same degree that I was growing in their esteem, I was growing concerned that I might never produce a commercial batch of tempeh fit for human consumption.

I began to worry about safety too. What if my tempeh made someone sick? I worried about my future customers, and I worried about giving tempeh a black eye just as it was starting to become the next granola. I left the co-op well after midnight each night and just lay in bed for hours as my stomach churned, and my brain offered up one disastrous scenario after another.

If that wasn't enough, I found myself with almost no personal life. My girlfriend Kim was in Santa Cruz finishing up her education degree, but even if she had been there, I wouldn't have had time for her. My mandolin rested quietly against a corner in the

Harvesting one of the first commercial batches of tempeh for Turtle Island Soy Dairy at Hope Co-op in 1981. Tempeh was a pioneering food in the infant plant-based protein market. The first commercial tempeh was made in Lincoln, Nebraska, five years earlier. *(The Tofurky Company)*

living room. My Frisbee-golf game suffered from neglect, especially my short game. I finally understood the first thing about running a business, which is that it's all encompassing, and it was turning out to be an expensive lesson.

It was in the midst of these growing worries that Robert from the co-op told me that the Small Business Administration offered free classes for people like me. I assumed that by "people like me," he meant new business owners. He might just as easily have meant "complete idiots." Both meanings applied.

"A lot of it is probably stuff you already understand," he said, "but there might be a few gaps they can fill in for you."

I told Robert I'd think about it, which meant I had too many other things to do.

"They're free," he said. "The classes."

That was different. Free was a price I could get behind. Robert told me where to go to sign up, and I told him again that I would think about it, but this time it meant that I would actually think about it. I still didn't consider myself a businessman, mostly because my idea of "businessman" was founded on the dorky business majors I'd encountered back in the day at Wittenberg University. However, I *was* running a business. It might be good to understand what that meant, exactly, before the entire operation turned into compost.

Planning for Success

Two weeks later, I cautiously stepped into the ballroom of a Portland hotel. I'd signed up for a one-day seminar specifically aimed at young entrepreneurs like myself, entitled "Planning for Success!" That seemed like a good start. The ballroom was in a mid-range hotel, but it seemed like the Taj Mahal to me. The hallways were lined wall to wall with plush carpet. The air matched the carpet with a fresh, floral scent—with just the slightest hint of industrial chemicals. I was twenty-nine years old and hadn't spent a single night at a hotel in America since I was in grade school and traveling with my parents.

A young woman greeted me with a big smile and a chirpy "Welcome!" She gave me a nametag to fill out and stick on my chest, which I did. Then she handed me a mimeographed sheet of paper, the program for the day, and pointed me to a folding table with Styrofoam cups and coffee. I poured myself a cup.

The ballroom was packed. Everyone seemed to be talking at once, gesturing with one hand and holding a cup of coffee with the other. I made my way to one of the last open chairs near the front of the room and took out the new ballpoint pen and notebook I'd bought just for the workshop. I was going to squeeze as much knowledge as possible out of this one-day workshop because afterwards I had to get back to the actual business of making tempeh that humans would like, or at least that they could consume without getting sick.

A large man in a sharp, black suit walked onto the stage in front me. *This*, I thought. *This* is was a businessman looks like— black suit, red tie, polished leather shoes, expensive haircut, big rings on both of his meaty hands, and then something else, a confidence that bordered on fierceness. The SBA is run by volunteers mostly, and most of them are retired businesspeople. This guy had been a vice president at Louisiana Pacific, a large timber firm that would later pay more than half a billion dollars to customers who installed one of its surprisingly mushroom-friendly siding products.

"I want to start," he boomed, instantly quieting the room. He smiled as the last voices stopped talking.

"I want to start," he said, "by asking two simple questions."

I wrote in my notebook: "2 questions."

"First, how many of you are here to save the world?"

My hand shot up. I didn't have to think about it. This guy got it. That was exactly why I was doing this. I wanted to give people a better alternative for protein, and I wanted to build a community around that work. The businessman looked at me with what I hoped was understanding but which might have been something else. I turned and looked behind me at the rest of the young entrepreneurs. Mine was the only raised hand. I lowered it.

"The second question," he said, "is how many of you are here . . ." He paused, leaned forward, and said, almost confidentially, "To make some *money*?"

The room erupted with laughter and applause. He stepped back and applauded the room for applauding him.

I'd been in business class for five minutes and already I was flunking out.

"I thought so!" he boomed. "I thought so."

He looked at me and smiled again.

"Let's get to work."

Early Production

On February 23, just as I was spending the last of my budgeted $2,500, Turtle Island made its first commercial batch of tempeh. The local reception was great. Six stores in Portland and the Hope Co-op in Forest Grove all agreed to take on this local product. My favorite restaurant, Center Family for Truth, was also a customer. I put the tempeh cakes into a cooler and delivered them in my little, "some-body-damage" delivery van, which I tried to park around the block from the store so as not to attract attention.

The stores themselves weren't exactly showrooms of modern retailing. Most featured worn wooden floors, second-hand refrigerators, five-gallon buckets of bulk items, and dreary lighting. The exceptions to this downscale look were Food Front Co-op and Nature's. Food Front was early to embrace my new product. I did several demos there, lugging in a card table and then sautéing tempeh with tamari in an electric skillet. I even did an interview on KBOO, Portland's community radio station. Things were looking up.

In that first month, I sold about ninety-six eight-ounce cakes of tempeh each week for seventy-four cents per cake. My materials cost thirty-two cents per unit, and at the minimum wage of $3.35 per hour—on those rare days when everything went well—my labor costs were thirty-five cents per unit. When I added in the cost of rent, gas, demos, marketing, and other costs, however, it turned out I was actually *paying* people to buy Turtle Island Tempeh.

In spite of that sad fact, it was still invigorating to actually *be* in business now. Gross sales of seventy-two dollars per week was a start, and it got me thinking about how to improve the operation. I set new goals for Turtle Island for the coming year:

- Nail down bookkeeping and basic tempeh making systems
- Do demos around town
- Train one or two apprentices
- Add new accounts
- Expand the tempeh line
- Grow sales to 200 pounds per week

While I was at it, I also set some long-term goals, which at age thirty meant the next two to five years:

- Grow tempeh sales to 500 pounds per week
- Produce tofu, soy milk, miso, and ice bean
- Move to a rural setting where I can run a farm, soy dairy, and outdoor school

These goals proved to be shockingly prophetic over the long haul. However, about five minutes after drafting this vision of the future, as I basked in the warm afterglow of all this forward thinking, one small flaw in my plans presented itself to the rational side of my brain. With a monthly gross income of less than $500, I was nowhere near outgrowing myself at Hope Co-op, much less being able to afford higher rent for bigger space elsewhere. Even if I found new space—where I could work during the daytime, which was what I really wanted—what bank was going to loan me the $5,000 I'd need to outfit that new space?

Ignoring that for the time being, I pressed ahead. Between making batches of tempeh late at night and visiting stores for demos or deliveries during the day, I began to search for my first employee. I started by writing up this job description, which I posted at the Co-op:

Hopefully, Turtle Island Soy Dairy will grow into a model cottage industry that can create financial support for an environmental school and farm as well as provide a living, non-government-supported monument to our dreams. Down the road, we are also excited about funding other soy dairies in other parts of the world where people need an inexpensive, delicious, high-protein food. Enough soybeans are now grown to provide every person on the planet with half of his or her daily protein needs, if eaten directly. So you see, we are a company of big dreams.

Together, we just could pull something off that the world needs to see. Useful people who don't whine when the government pulls the rug out from under their feet but who have the gumption to plunge headfirst into an unknown pond. And if we land on our heads—so what?

Amazingly, my call for fellow dreamers to join this noble mission turned up no one. Maybe I shouldn't have added this line:

Only hardy, pie-in-the-sky dreamer lunatics need apply. To be honest, folks, while we will surely get fed and clothed from our work, there just ain't no money in it no how for nobody. Salary: $3.00/hour (when available).

What further complicated my under-funded and misunderstood mission was an underdeveloped market for plant-based proteins. In the conventional supermarkets of North America, there were no plant-based proteins or meat alternatives of any kind—no tofu, no tempeh, no plant-based milks, cheeses, or yogurts—no *nothing*. The only marketplace for my wares was in a small but growing collection of co-ops, health food stores, and alternative restaurants. It was going to be hard to grow sales without some growth in the market.

Fortunately, I didn't care. Sure, I wanted to make enough money to live on, but money wasn't the primary goal. I was on a mission—just ask the guy from the SBA workshop. I was introducing America to a new food, and once people tried it, they would beat a path to the Hope Co-op in no time. I just *knew* if people just tried it—even once—they would fall in love with it at first bite like I had.

It was exciting to be there too, in this world of business. I knew I was in over my head, but I was gradually becoming less stupid about it. It would take me years to figure this out, but it turned out that I had a lot of assets that balanced out my many short-comings. I was determined. I was a creative problem-solver. I was adventurous. During my eight years as a wandering naturalist, I had fine-tuned the art of living on the cheap. Perhaps the most important asset was that I learned quickly from my mistakes, so my lack of understanding became a great teacher. I gave myself a crash course in business by making mistake after mistake.

Through March, I continued to make just barely enough tempeh to supply my little Portland market. It was exciting to deliver to stores and find an empty shelf that needed restocking. I fell into a groove of making tempeh a couple of days in the beginning of the week, storing those frozen eight-ounce cakes in a cooler, and delivering them towards the end of the week.

I also hired my first part-time employee, my old friend Belinda, who I had first met at the Farm in 1976 when she was pregnant with her first daughter, Molly. Belinda was a strong woman with a big heart. She and husband Garry were the main movers behind the fledgling outdoor school and camp at the Cherry Grove Center. One day while driving into town, Belinda pointed to a new dairy barn and said, "That's a cow concentration camp. The cows spend all their days in there, never seeing the light of day." It was one of the first times I ever stopped to think about the plight of farm animals.

Belinda was no "pie-in-the-sky dreamer lunatic," but she believed in the mission and was willing to help with production. This meant that I had to increase sales just to cover my overhead, but it also meant that I could put more time into developing new lines and adding more accounts.

The First Break

On April Fools' Day, I got a call from a new natural food distributor in Portland, Applegate Foods. A California distributor had gone broke, and Applegate was hoping to take over their business—including tempeh. They'd heard good things from stores about Turtle Island's tempeh line, so they wanted to get us into their system. Starting in June, they told me, they'd need a thousand pounds of tempeh each week. I couldn't believe it—a thousand pounds! That night I could hardly sleep, but this time it was from excitement about the future, not dread about the present.

My excitement, however, was short-lived. The very next day I found out that a local tofu maker, Colony Soy Dairy, which was already selling tofu to Applegate, was planning to go into the tempeh business. The buyer for Applegate called back and said he didn't know quite what to do. He suggested that I set up a meeting with Colony and "work things out," which meant "partner up with Colony so my problem goes away."

On the surface, partnering with Colony wasn't the worst idea in the world. Colony had a bigger space of their own, had some good tofu-making equipment, and was starting to sell tofu in a revolutionary water pack. That meant that stores like Hope Co-op wouldn't have to scoop the bean curd out of five-gallon buckets and package it in Chinese restaurant take-out boxes. They also didn't have to work during the night, which might have been the most attractive thing of all for me.

It all sounded like some kind of destiny, but something inside of me rebelled. When I met with them, they talked about how easy it was to make tempeh. This told me that they hadn't actually tried to make tempeh in commercial quantities, which was anything but easy. Perhaps more importantly, I'd already grown attached to my little mission-based brand and to the dreams that I'd sketched out about what this business could do for me and for the world. Colony didn't have the same vision. I mean, my business was named for Turtle Island, and they were named for colonies. That's not a great match.

After that meeting with Colony, I decided to double down on Turtle Island. I started by expanding my tempeh line with two new products. I invented the country's first "five grain tempeh," which was made with organic soybeans, millet, rice, sesame, and sunflower seeds. Then I created a sausage-shaped tempeh cake that came with a blend of *herbs de Provence* that I called "Tempehroni."

Looking back, I see now that Tempehroni was an early ancestor of Tofurky. It was a playful name, and the labeling was playful too. My artist friend Jan drew me a happy and weird soybean chef tossing a pizza crust into the air. A thermometer told shoppers the spiciness "Tempehture." Although almost everyone had no idea what tempeh or Tempehroni was, we tried to hook them into trying it out by making them smile.

With new products in place, the next thing I did was hit the streets of Portland hard, going to more stores and more restaurants looking for expanded distribution of Turtle Island tempeh products. The most advanced natural foods retailer in Portland was a chain of two stores called "Nature's." I was intimidated by their new produce coolers and display cases and fancy lighting, which were a far cry from the co-op vibe of natural food stores back then. When I walked in, though, the buyer was welcoming and friendly.

"We were wondering when you would come around to see us," he said. "Do you have any other products besides the Soy Tempeh? We're having trouble filling up our shelves!"

As a matter of fact, I *did* have other products besides Soy Tempeh.

You be the judge!

TURTLE ISLAND SOY DAIRY presents:
TEMPEH
·THREE WAYS!

TURTLE ISLAND, Gary Snyder tells us, is the name some of the original settlers gave to this continent. And now, tempeh has come to Turtle Island bringing with it the promise of a new day. For within this promise is the opportunity to bring to the American diet a low on the food chain, high protein food that is quick and easy to prepare and tasty and nutritious to eat.

We are so excited about the food potential of tempeh that we feel it merits our full attention, experimentation and promotion. We make no other products. We are now pleased to invite you to be the judge of 3 of the ways that we have learned to prepare this amazing food.

Soy Tempeh   Five Grain   Tempehroni
good old soy   *the complementary protein tempeh*   *soy tempeh with herbs*

-traditional soy tempeh made from organically grown soybeans

-our own unique blend of millet, rice, sesame seeds, sunflower seeds and soybeans

-soy tempeh incubated with organically grown herbs in a sausage shaped roll. Great on pizza or in other Italian foods!

To help acquaint your customers with our tempeh, we offer the following promotional aids:

*TEMPEH INFORMATION AND RECIPES BROCHURE--nutritional facts and some of our favorite basic recipes.

*RECIPE OF THE MONTH CARD--each month we send all of our accounts a pad containing a new tempeh recipe!

*COOKING CLASSES AND DEMOS--a two hour cooking class taught by expert tempeh cooks. We also do in-store demos. Call or write for details.

*PROMOTIONAL MEDIA PACKET--copies of tempeh articles from newspapers and magazines including an article on Turtle Island from a recent issue of the OREGONIAN. Available on request.

It is a great pleasure and alot of fun doing something that we truely believe in here in the 80's. If we can be of help to you in any way, please contact us:
TURTLE ISLAND SOY DAIRY, Route 2 Box 73, Gaston, Oregon 97119 (503) 985-7908.

First Tempeh brochure; typed on an electric typewriter. Big print was in press on letters. *(Seth Tibbott)*

67

The addition of Five Grain Tempeh and Tempehroni brought new interest in the brand. Stores started calling Applegate and demanding Turtle Island products. I didn't know about this at the time, but a few stores, including Hope Co-op and Food Front, told Applegate that they wouldn't buy Colony tempeh from them.

In the end, my new products and hard work paid off. The buyer from Applegate called and told me that they'd decided to go with Turtle Island instead of Colony. That meant we'd expand our reach from Portland to Seattle, Salem, Eugene, and Northern California. I could finally see a path to profitability that was not paved by crazed tempeh fans beating a path to my door. The market for this awesome, low-on-the-food-chain protein seemed to be starting off on its granola-like trajectory.

As exciting as this was, there was one small problem. With a maximum production capacity of three hundred pounds of tempeh per week, my tiny shop in the Hope Co-op wouldn't be able to meet the new demand. I'd need to find a new production facility, with new equipment, where we could work during the day, night, or both if necessary. Turtle Island needed its own home, and a new home was going to cost a lot more money than I had in my quickly disappearing reserves.

Soon after the Applegate call, I was running a demo at the new Nature's store in Northeast Portland. A tall, long-haired man with a heavy beard stopped by for a tempeh sample. He was keenly interested in the product and peppered me with questions. He turned out to be Alexander Lyon, PhD, a microbiologist and former resident of the Farm—the same Alexander Lyon, PhD, who set up the first tempeh starter shop in the US and also helped build the first soy dairy on the Farm. In fact, Alex had worked with the leading tempeh researchers at Cornell and at the government's Northern Regional Research Lab in Peoria, Illinois, to obtain tempeh starter culture that he could propagate commercially. At that point in time, he probably knew more about making tempeh than anyone in the entire country—and he was looking for work.

By summer, Turtle Island was grossing about $600 per month, which was great, but it wasn't enough that I could really afford to pay Alex or Belinda very much. Alex signed on anyway. I decided that I would make it work with more growth in sales. Having him there also meant I could spend more time looking for a new place to set up a "Tempeh 2.0" shop—and the money I'd need to raise to set up that shop.

That summer, Turtle Island hit an all-time weekly high with a single order from Applegate for four hundred pounds of tempeh. My little Tempeh 1.0 shop at Hope Co-op was busting at the seams. I was busting at the seams too. Never in all my years as a naturalist had I worked as hard as I worked that summer. There were days when I was so tired by the time I got the tempeh set up at midnight that I'd grab a sleeping bag out of the delivery van and spend the rest of the night bivouacked in Hope Co-op's little kids' area next to the kitchen. The rug was surprisingly comfortable, and the hum of the refrigerator's compressor was as soothing a sound as I've ever heard.

One night, though, I was so tired that when I took off for home, I left a pot of beans on a stove burner all night and almost burnt the co-op down. Robert came in the next morning to find the co-op filled with smoke. He called the fire department, and they raced down to clear things out. Fortunately, there was no serious damage. Robert didn't need to tell me it was time for me to move on after that. We both understood that it was somewhat *past* time for Turtle Island to find a home of its own.

From then on, I left most of the production work to Belinda and Alex and spent a couple of days every week on the prowl for new shop space. I knew it needed to be at least five hundred square feet and close enough to Portland for weekly deliveries. I

Turtle Island's first tempeh incubator, a repurposed old refrigerator. *(The Tofurky Company)*

also knew it had to have affordable rent, by which I meant "dirt cheap." Those two needs were always in conflict with each other no matter where I looked. However, in a universe of infinite possibilities, I figured that such a place must exist. I just needed to find it.

20/20 HINDSIGHT:
The Sound of One Hand Raising

When I raised my hand at that SBA seminar and voted for "save the world" instead of "make some money," I thought for just a second that I was the only person who had gotten that question right. It didn't take me long to realize that I'd gotten it wrong. Mr.

SBA Businessman made that clear enough. However, looking back at that moment from where I stand now, I can see that the actual correct answer is to raise both of your hands. You should try to save the world *and* make some money.

For any world-saving business to succeed, it needs to make money just like any other business does. This sounds painfully obvious now, but I was painfully *oblivious* back then. I thought it was enough to save the world, that people would respect that and give me their money. Maybe a few did too, out of respect for my mission or pity for my obliviousness. However, in the long run, it wasn't enough just to have a good mission. I also had to become a lot less stupid about business so that I could pursue my mission by making some money.

If I had followed my friend Bill's advice and actually read *Small Time Operator*, my early years in business would have been more fruitful. Even a little bit of business know-how up front would have helped me to understand the ins and outs of pricing, margins, record-keeping, and a thousand other aspects of running a successful business.

I probably should have taken a business class or two before launching Turtle Island. It would not have been that hard to find help from the Small Business Association or the local community college or correspondence classes, which were a thing back then. "Correspondence" is what we used to call letters that were written on paper and sent to other people through the postal system. Anyway, I probably cost myself $100,000 over the first ten years by not knowing the things I would have learned from taking a single Intro to Business class back at Wittenberg University.

Once you're making money, you can hire people who have the know-how you still lack. You can't hire passion for the mission, but you can hire everything else. In the early days of bootstrapping, though, it's all on you to know how to run a successful business. So learn as much as you can as quickly as you can—and maybe learn something before you raise *either* hand—or else you'll end up like me having to learn it all from your mistakes. Build your business to change the world, but don't be an idiot about it. Try to make some money too.

SCALING UP

I n which I scour the Portland area for concrete floors with drains, am showered by dead spider parts in a windowless and doorless basement, glimpse Nirvana through dirty windows, invite my big brother to look out for me, and serve tempeh to a room full of unsmiling conservatives. As a business, Turtle Island outgrows its first home and continues to prove the concept I naively envisioned from a bathtub. It now requires more production and better space to meet the steadily growing demand for tempeh.

Bootstrappers, moving to a new production space is one of the most important and perilous decisions your company will face. You're basically betting the business on finding the right space for the right amount of new production at the right price. If you overestimate the market for new product, the high overhead and debt can sink the business no matter how good the product is. If you underestimate the market, you might be going through another costly search in just a few years—and that can sink you, too.

The Need to Grow

By June of 1981, the need for new space had become the biggest challenge in making Turtle Island viable. The business was growing steadily, but I was starting to get sick on a regular basis from overwork—something that had never been a problem until then—and also from working such strange hours, night and day. For the business to keep growing and for me to not flame out, Turtle Island needed more space, better equipment, and a day shift. Just as importantly, it needed to find space it could afford.

This was more than just a business need. My personal life was a mess. I had almost no time for friends or music. My girlfriend Kim had just graduated from college and was ready to roam to the far corners of the earth and have some adventures. I *so* wanted to go with her—and that had been my plan, after all, to work six months and then take six months off—but there was no way I could leave this newborn business in anyone else's hands. It needed my own careful attention just about every day.

Was it still worth it to run my own business? That's one of those questions that never really goes away. The numbers change over the life of a business, but the questions stay the same. It is worth it? Where do I go to get money for growth? How do I balance my work and personal life? How big should this business be? Is it time for me to get out?

That's what I was asking myself after just six months of being in business, and I was pretty sure I knew what the answers were too. Yes, it was still worth it. My brand was growing, so I had to assume that prosperity wasn't too far away. I just needed to find better space to meet the demand for more tempeh. Once I found the space, I could talk to my brother Bob about investing in new equipment for the company. Then I could work shorter hours *and* produce more tempeh. With better space and better equipment, I could finally get my work and personal lives back into equilibrium.

That was my plan for the second half of the first year in business:

1. Keep growing the business.
2. Find a place for the Tempeh 2.0 shop.
3. Secure financing to fill the space with new equipment.
4. Start to enjoy the benefits of working for myself.

That all seemed easy enough to do, especially now that I'd learned so much about business from making every possible mistake for the previous six months.

The Room to Grow

Leaving most of the production work to my two part-time employees, Belinda and Alex, I began devoting at least a couple of days each week to the search for space. The place had to have concrete floors, preferably with drains. It had to have sturdy, washable walls and come with all the usual utilities. We needed to have at least 500 square feet, probably more. Oh, and the rent couldn't be more than $400 per month, and hopefully quite a bit less. My dream was to find a piece of land out in the country that had a house big enough for me to sublet rooms, an outbuilding for the tempeh shop, and land where I could grow vegetables and compost all of the tempeh that I ruined.

Within a few weeks, I'd visited a dozen promising and not-so-promising locations, but each one either cost too much to rent or would have cost too much to fix up. Some of them were just too weird.

Not too far from the Hope Co-op, I found an old concrete building with floor drains that had once been the "milking parlor" for what used to be a dairy farm. It had some utilities, and the sweet older woman who lived beside it would be my landlord. She was willing to meet me on price, possibly because she was a bit lonely, just wanting to have someone around. It was big enough and in a good location, and I liked the landlord, but getting it up to speed for tempeh production would have required massive amounts of cleaning and improvements to the building. I had to say no.

Also near the co-op, and within an easy drive to Portland, was an empty and affordable space in a new industrial park. Here was a thousand square feet at a price I could afford, but when I say "empty," I mean really empty—no plumbing, no electricity, no nothing. It would also take a huge investment of capital I didn't have, and the would-be landlord had no interest in helping with that.

I found a welding shop on a beautiful farm about eighteen miles from Portland. There was a cozy little rental house with three bedrooms on the property too. This fit nicely with my long-term dream of running a tempeh shop on land that could also serve as some kind of small, community-run environmental center. Again, though, it was going to take a lot of money and hard work to put a food-processing plant into a welding shop, and I'd be making that major investment in someone else's property.

Getting a little more desperate, I even checked out a basement in the middle of Portland. It had the floor drain I needed but no clean walls for food processing. In fact, it had no windows or doors, either. The only way to get supplies in or out was by way of a freight elevator that opened up onto the sidewalk, the kind of thing that people fall into when running from the police in movies. Worst of all, there was a speedometer shop in the building above it. Every time they calibrated the speedometers, the ceiling shook violently and bits of dust and dead spider parts sifted down from the ceiling.

That place was wrong, of course, but nothing else was quite right, either.

Meanwhile, the orders for tempeh were getting bigger, and after my low-grade fire at Hope Co-op, the managers there were getting impatient. Finding nothing that worked in the area, I turned my thoughts in another direction, to the small town of Trout Lake, Washington. A handful of friends from my wandering naturalist days had bought cheap land in the area and were starting to build their own cabins and houses there. The town was nestled at the base of 12,000-foot Mount Adams, and although it was ninety miles from Portland, which would make deliveries harder, they were a magical ninety miles through the stunningly scenic Columbia Gorge.

Another reason to head for the remote village of Trout Lake was the tempeh itself. From all the reading I had done, I'd learned that the best tempeh in Indonesia came not from the big cities but from rural areas that had more access to clean air and water. Specifically, the small village of Malang in East Java was famous for its tempeh. The tempeh shops in Malang made fresh tempeh every day and delivered it to the city of Surabaya in microbuses. That could be me, I thought, with my little Datsun delivery van that might as easily be called a microbus.

I made a dozen trips to Trout Lake and the surrounding area that summer, but once again, nothing quite worked. It was always either too small, too run down, or too expensive. For a month in the summer, I even made plans to buy a second-hand trailer and turn it into a portable tempeh shop that I could park on friends' land until I found a place of my own. I still have the plans for that portable tempeh shop, if you'd like to see them or possibly buy them. As much as I liked Trout Lake in the summer, the locals were also pretty direct in telling me about winters. At a 2,000-foot elevation, the valley gets plenty of snow and ice that make transportation in and out of town a dicey proposition.

By fall I was no closer to finding Tempeh 2.0 than I had been in June. Orders were ramping up, Kim was getting impatient with my lack of personal time, money was running out, and between my search for space and running the business, I was exhausted. I just couldn't see myself going forward with *any* of these options. As much as I hated to admit it, and in spite of warnings from my friend Robert at Hope Co-op and "the Bible," *Small Time Operator*, it seemed like my best and only option would be to partner up with the tofu-makers at Colony.

Tempeh Nirvana

Sometime in early October, I drove down the White Salmon Valley from Trout Lake after what I supposed would be the last of my searches for space in Klickitat County. It just wasn't going to work out, I thought. I wasn't going to find the right space, and Turtle Island probably wasn't going to survive as a business for too much longer. I was feeling pretty low.

On my drive down the beautiful White Salmon River, I pulled off in the little town of Husum to admire the falls where the river cuts through a big formation of basalt. These falls are famous now in the kayaking and rafting world, but back then they were just beautiful to look at. I walked out onto the highway bridge and leaned over the railing and stared at them. The warm October sun gave the town a pleasant piney smell as it worked its way through the Ponderosa pines on either side of the river.

Husum was even smaller than Trout Lake. It consisted of a café, a church, a fire station, a post office, and seventeen houses.

The biggest building in town was an abandoned elementary school just beyond where I'd parked. As I walked back to my sad little Datsun, I saw what sort of looked like an old "For Sale" sign taped to the front door. I fired up the Datsun and drove over for a closer look. It was a "For Sale" sign, and judging from the general decay of the duct tape that held it in place, it had been there for a long time.

I wandered around the building to peek into the windows. There were four empty classrooms on one wing of the L-shaped building. On the other wing, there was a gym, an office full of old boxes, and—after I'd rubbed off enough grime to peer inside—the tempeh shop of my dreams, exactly what I'd been looking for, tempeh Nirvana.

I stared in wonder at a small industrial kitchen that was exactly the right size for an expanded Turtle Island. It came with two stainless steel sinks that would easily hold our baking trays of soybeans. The concrete floors were covered with clean red tile and had not one but two floor drains. A stainless-steel exhaust hood shined above an industrial oven and grill. The most incredible thing, though, was that there were not one but two storage rooms off to one side, and either one was the ideal size for an incubator that could handle 300 pounds of tempeh at a time. It was perfect. It was like the elementary school architects from 1953 had time-traveled to me in the future and asked if the kitchen looked all right to me.

"One storage room or two?" they might have asked.

"Oh," I might have said, "Let's go with two."

"Two it is!"

There was a phone number to call on the For Sale sign, but it was a Sunday so nobody would have picked up on the other end. It was also 1981, so I didn't have a cell phone and couldn't have called anyway except from a pay phone in White Salmon or

Hood River. Instead of calling on my nonexistent cell phone or checking out a nonexistent *Zillow* listing, I did an analog information search by walking across the highway to Don and Betty's Café. An old-timer sat at the front counter reading a month-old newspaper.

I asked about the school, and without looking up from the paper, he told me that the school had been empty for the last seven years after logging collapsed in Klickitat County and the school district in White Salmon had to shut it down for lack of students.

"Why isn't anyone using it?"

"Well," he said, scratching his neck. "Some tried."

"And?"

"Tits up," he said.

He looked up from the paper and gave me a look that was clearly measuring me to find out how long it would take for me to go tits up too. His frown suggested months more than years.

I didn't care. The school was perfect, a palace of opportunity. The only question I had was if the school board would consider renting instead of selling. I guess I also wondered how much they would charge for rent. I'd only budgeted $400 a month for rent, and that seemed like a pretty big stretch for this much space.

On the way back to Forest Grove, I mapped out the Tempeh 2.0 configuration. Then I mapped out how I'd rent out the classrooms to local businesses, including the graphic design company a few other friends were starting in Trout Lake. I turned my thoughts to the gym and scheduled pick-up basketball nights and gym-hockey nights. It was perfect. The closer I got to Forest Grove, the more I was convinced that this school would be the new home for Turtle Island—and so much more. After all the misses and near misses over the past three months, I had finally found the right place.

The next morning, I called the White Salmon School District offices, and they put me through to the superintendent, Rick.

"No," he said. "We're not looking to rent it. We want to sell it."

That was crushing news.

"Fifty thousand," he said.

That was even more crushing news. There was no way I could buy it, not even if they sold it to me on contract with no money down. Rick was friendly, though, and without any prompting from me, he told me that the building had been sitting empty without upkeep or tenants for a long time now. There'd been a couple of different locals who'd tried to make small craft businesses work there, but they'd failed. Klickitat County, after all, was one of the poorest counties in Washington. He also warned me that there was no heat in the building because the boiler was broken.

My ears perked up at that news. Having no heat was the building equivalent of a car having "some body damage." Maybe this was something I *could* afford—if I could convince them to rent to me.

Rick kept talking. He told me the building was 13,000 square feet, all told, with a nice full gym that had a stage on one end.

"Tile floor," he said, "but nice."

He told me again that nobody had been in the building for quite a long time and that it would be good to have someone in there, even on a rental basis, since it's bad to just leave a building empty like that. The more we talked, the more he talked himself into renting the school to me after all. Finally, I asked him if I could at least get a look inside.

"Sure," he said. "We can do that."

"If we did rent to you," he added, "I'd hope it might lead to a purchase."

"It sure might," I told him.

A week later, the facilities manager for the school district met me at the school and let me in. What had looked promising from the outside looked even better on the inside. The hallways had a faint, musty odor to them, but what really stood out was how nice and clean they were. The boys' and girls' bathrooms seemed to be in good shape. I was especially excited to see the full-length basketball court in the gym. Basketball was my favorite sport, and as Rick had said, the linoleum tile floor was still in good shape. All it needed was a good mopping. This could be home for Wednesday night basketball in Greater Husum.

As expected for October, the building was a bit cold, but I figured the rooms could all be individually heated with space heaters. I'd be able to heat the kitchen with a new kettle. The new incubator would be like Miami Beach with a steady eighty-eight degrees, so I figured I could always go in there to warm up. I tried to play it cool with the facilities guy, but it wasn't easy. I could barely contain my excitement.

As soon as I got back to Forest Grove, I called Rick back and told him I'd like to present a proposal to the school board at his earliest convenience. He seemed surprised, possibly because he'd thought he'd been talking me *out* of this idea, but he put me on the agenda for the school board meeting in November. I thanked him and hung up. This was it, I thought. This was Nirvana for Turtle Island. I was either going to figure out a way to make this work or die trying.

Family Investment

To move from my jury-rigged set-up at Hope Co-op to a real production plant in the Husum school, I would have to do more than just talk my way into leasing the building at a price I could afford.

I'd also have to move better equipment into the school's kitchen in order to produce enough tempeh to pay the rent, meet the growing demand, and cover the wages for my two part-time employees. While I was pretty sure I could scrape together the rent from increased sales, I didn't have the money for the equipment.

I was not a good risk for any investor at this time. Although I had become somewhat less stupid as a businessman by the fall of 1981, my education was a slow one that came mostly from correcting a surprisingly wide variety of mistakes. In those first ten months, I'd made a lot of mistakes, but there were still pristine meadows of stupid that I had yet to explore.

Years later I asked my friend and mentor Robert at Hope Co-op whether he would have invested in Turtle Island.

"Oh no," he said, smiling, "No. You've done just fine for yourself, but I wouldn't have backed you back then. You were pretty dense in the ways of business."

I only had only one option for funding a move to Husum, and it was the same one that is the only option for a lot of bootstrappers—friends or family money. As soon as I'd hung up the phone after talking with Rick, I got a new dial tone and called my brother Bob in Maryland.

"Bob," I said, "How'd you like to come out to Oregon for a visit?"

Before he could answer that question, I added, "I think I've found the perfect home for Turtle Island, and I'd like you to check it out. I think this would be a great investment."

I admitted to Bob that I wasn't making a lot of money—yet. Sales were around $1,300 per month in a good month, so I could only pay Belinda and Alex small amounts as contractors rather than employees. I wasn't paying myself anything yet and was living instead on my dwindling savings from the big summer in Alaska. But I told Bob that if things kept going the way they'd been going, it wouldn't be long before I reached my goal of paying myself $1,000 a month.

I told Bob that there were a lot of hopeful signs too. The mission of bringing this eco-friendly protein to the American public resonated with lots of the people I met. I had given demos and cooking classes all over the Portland area, turning hundreds of potential customers on to tempeh. The company had drawn some media attention to itself. Through my deal with Applegate, I'd expanded my reach beyond Portland to new markets in Oregon, Washington, and Northern California. Perhaps most importantly, I'd learned how to scale up my little hobby of making one-pound batches of tempeh to making hundred-pound batches. By October, I was consistently making high-quality product too, much to the dismay of the local towhee community.

Bob listened patiently.

I told him that Belinda and Alex were now trained and capable tempeh makers, and that I could easily see us tripling our production as demand for tempeh grew—as it had been growing and would surely continue to grow. The only missing piece was a Tempeh 2.0 shop, and I was pretty sure I'd found the right place in Husum.

Now I needed to outfit it with about $6,000 in equipment and kitchen improvements. A bank loan was out of the question, of course. I had very few records in any traditional sense of "record-keeping," so I didn't have any way to show even the most compassionate and supportive banker that Turtle Island was a viable business, even though I was pretty sure that it was. On top of that, the only collateral I could offer was a broad selection of pots and pans and a Datsun wagon that kept its driver-side door closed with a bungee cord.

If I was going to move forward, then, I needed an angel investor who believed in me and my ability to grow this business to a point where I could make good on the loan. I paused. Bob said nothing. I needed someone who was willing to overlook my current lack of a business track record in the plant-based protein market and rely instead on my successful work selling animal-based protein in the form of Chesapeake Bay crabs back in the summer of 1964.

Bob laughed, but he said he wasn't sure if he could be my angel investor. He'd just been laid off from his well-paying job at the National Bureau of Standards outside Washington, D.C. He'd worked there as an environmental psychologist, so it wasn't just environmental education that got cut by the Reagan White House. It was environmental *anything*. He told me he only had about $8,000 in his retirement account at the moment, but that since he was out of work, he supposed he could pull some out of the account.

The other thing that concerned Bob was that while he had been working steadily at dependable jobs throughout the 1970s, I'd been drifting all over the country from one seasonal job to the next. I'd spent almost as much time on trips to Mexico or the swamps of Florida in search of the ivory-billed woodpecker, a bird that almost everyone agreed was extinct, as I had spent working. Was this tempeh thing going to be just another passing phase in a life built on passing phases?

The Tibbott family history also worked against me. As far as Bob knew, no Tibbotts had ever started their own businesses. That point didn't seem quite as fair as the others, but it was true. I would be the first.

All that being said, Bob did have the time to come for a visit, being laid off as he was, so he agreed to fly out and take a closer look. Bob spent almost a month with me in Oregon. He helped me make tempeh during my late-night shift at the Hope Co-op. He visited the stores that carried Turtle Island products. He came to Husum and took a tour of the school with me and the facilities guy from White Salmon.

In spite of his lingering doubts, and possibly because of his life-long habit of looking out for his little brother, Bob agreed that if I could get into the school, he would loan me the money I needed to equip that beautiful school kitchen. My little business benefitted from the generosity of a lot of people in those early days. No one helped more than my big brother.

The Pitch

When it came time to make my pitch to the White Salmon School Board, the person I felt most positively about was Superintendent Rick. I could tell he liked me and that he was open to my ideas. Klickitat County in general was and mostly still is firmly conservative in its politics. Rick, though, had come to town from a school district in Southern California. He was a progressive thinker who was open to new ideas and also one of the few residents of Klickitat County who had actually been inside a natural foods store.

The rest of the board ranged from ultra-conservative to just conservative in their political leanings and openness to what we used to call the "counterculture." In 1981, tempeh was virtually unknown even to most of the vegetarians in liberal Portland, so I knew it would be a strange business indeed for this board made up of loggers, ranchers, and local businesspeople. As my Aunt Rosie might have said, these were meat-eating Americans who would have zero interest in moldy soybeans.

The November school board meeting was held in the old concrete high school building that had been converted into school district offices and a community center. The five board members and Rick sat on metal folding chairs around a Formica table. Bob and I sat off to one side while they debated how to put a new roof on the district's only remaining elementary school. When it was my turn to present, I passed around a brochure I'd typed up that described tempeh. Then I offered them some samples.

I'd prepared two tempeh dishes. The first was a simple appetizer of thin, marinated tempeh strips that I'd sautéed in safflower oil. I served these with a barbecue sauce on the side for dipping. Delicious. The second dish was a cold tempeh salad that looked like a chicken salad to the untrained eye. Conscious of how weird this product must have sounded to them, I tried to put them at ease by dressing for success—that is, like the locals. I wore a button-down plaid shirt that I'd picked up at Goodwill, a pair of jeans without any holes in them, and a pair of olive-green L.L.Bean sneakers that felt more serious than my usual Chuck Taylor high-tops. I couldn't tell if my wardrobe upgrade calmed any of their nerves, but it certainly amused Bob.

While I told the board about my plans for the building and how this would bring jobs to the county, especially with the anticipated growth, the board members snacked quietly on my protein from the future. I tried to read the room. The chairman of the board, a prominent orchardist, was the most conservative member of the bunch, and I could tell from his frown that he wasn't impressed with the tempeh or me. The local dentist and the wife of a man who owned several pharmacies in the county appeared to be at least neutral. They were eating the tempeh I'd set in front of them, but they did so cautiously. The fifth board member, Margaret, who was described to me later as "more of a conservative moderate than a moderate conservative," was actually smiling as she wolfed down her tempeh.

When I was done, the chairman got right to the point.

"Say we rent the school to you," he said. "How much can you afford to pay?"

I didn't know what to say. My budgeted amount of $400 per month from the start of summer was sixteen times what I was paying at the co-op, and by November, it was becoming clear to me that even $400 was still pretty unrealistic. That tends to happen with a number you pull out of thin air.

This was a negotiation, though. I could see that. So I started low. "How about $150 a month?"

They all stopped eating my tasty tempeh dishes at once. At first there was just silence, and then there was the awkward sound of heavily constructed hindquarters adjusting their position in old, squeaky metal chairs. The chairman folded his arms and looked up at the dingy ceiling. I felt stupid, like a teenager who'd just asked for his first pack of condoms and pronounced the word "conDOME." I looked over at Bob, who was looking at the tile floor. This was going to be ugly, I thought.

Then Margaret, the woman who seemed to really like tempeh, gave a little laugh. Everyone looked at her. I was pretty sure this was the end of our negotiation.

"Oh, for crying out loud," she said. "I say we take it."

The others just looked at her.

"What have we got to lose?"

In my many years as a businessman, I have heard a lot of different people say a lot of different things. I've never heard anything sweeter than those words. The dentist and pharmacist's wife eventually nodded in agreement, and although the orchardist shook his head at the idea, in the end, he didn't object. The school was mine for $150 a month!

This year had begun with unexpected generosity and kindness from the managers of the Hope Co-op, and now it was drawing to a close with this generous vote of confidence from the White Salmon School Board. This new home in Husum was the perfect place that I'd been searching for since spring. The low rent allowed me to survive through some *pretty lean years* as my little business waited for the market for tempeh and plant-based foods to ripen. The school board's generosity came back to them too. Renting the building to me meant that I had to get everything back to working order in the school, and that made the property attractive enough that years later they were able to sell it. That's what I call a good deal—not a matter of winners and losers but one in which all parties get something good out of it.

The Husum School in 2019, now a Klickitat County firehouse. *(Sue Tibbott)*

Turtle Island 2.0

After sealing the deal for the school, Bob and I headed down the chilly Columbia Gorge toward Forest Grove. A cold November headwind knocked my little Datsun around, and a light rain began to fall. I was so excited that I couldn't stop talking, just trying to process what this good fortune was going to mean for Turtle Island.

This was big, I told Bob. This was huge. We'd buy new, bigger equipment. We'd roll out new, refreshed packaging—and lots of it too. I laughed. We were going to sell so much tempeh! But making more tempeh was just the start. I had a whole school to myself. I only needed the kitchen and one of the classrooms for Turtle Island.

I had the gym to offer to my wandering naturalist friends in Trout Lake and the Husumites in those seventeen houses. I could just imagine how a new community might form around Turtle Island. We couldn't really do an environmental education camp at the school, but we were close to so much wilderness—maybe this could become the basecamp for something that took kids out there. I talked and talked all the way down the Gorge until we passed Multnomah Falls and I finally looked over at Bob. He was fast asleep.

At the same time, I could also see that my dream of working six months on and then taking six months off was a pretty dumb idea and always had been. There was my big brother, sleeping in the cab beside me, and there was me, about to borrow most of his retirement savings to fund this leap forward. It wasn't just a matter of me wanting to see my baby grow because it was so cool. Now it *had* to grow because I had to pay him back. I was going to have to work even harder to make sure that happened.

Even so, I couldn't stop grinning. This was going to be so great.

To no one's surprise but my own, the move to Husum proved to be more expensive and involved more than I foresaw on that drive home from the board meeting. Because the building had been sitting empty for so long, I had to run new lines for water, electricity, and gas. That was a good way to meet some of the local trades people, but it wasn't cheap. Getting the kitchen up and running took more time than I'd planned, especially when it came to turning one of those six-by-ten storage rooms into a high-volume soybean incubator.

I spent months haunting the used restaurant equipment warehouses of Portland for a hamburger mixer, a stainless-steel extractor, a small walk-in freezer, and the centerpiece of the whole operation, a steam-jacketed kettle for boiling the beans. It took me more than a month to haggle the owner down to $1,200 for that kettle, and then—I am not making this up—when I showed up the next day to pick it up, his wife met me at the door and told me that her husband had died that very night, which meant that both the kettle and the rest of his estate were now in probate.

"You're kidding me," I said, which I realize now was not the right thing to say.

She wasn't kidding, however, and I would have lost the kettle and month of haggling if she hadn't agreed to take my check anyway and send me home with that part of the estate.

One month of preparation become two months, and two months become four months, but in spite of the slow pace and unexpected costs, Turtle Island 2.0 was finally ready for production by March 1982. For the final push forward, I called up all my friends and invited them to the school for a kind of moving-in party. I directed folks as they moved in bags of soybeans, boxes of new tempeh packaging, and some of the final pieces of equipment. Then we brought out the beer, cooked up some first-rate Turtle Island tempeh, and had a little thanksgiving feast there in my new gym.

Turtle Island was nowhere close to being profitable, of course, but on that night in March, it sure *felt* profitable. I could see a great new future stretching out in front of me. I was in *business*, man. Turtle Island 2.0 was going to be so great.

After the feast, as my friends cleared away the folding tables and chairs so we could play some basketball, I noticed that off in a corner, a woman was sitting with her head down. Two other women were apparently comforting her. When I walked over to them, I saw that they were comforting Kim.

"It's so small," she said, waving her arm to indicate the gym, I suppose, or Turtle Island, or Husum—my new life. "It's just so *small*." And then her tears started to fall.

There was Kim, finally done with college and ready to roam the world, to be at large. And here was me, barely a year removed from my own days of wandering and getting ready to settle down in tiny Husum for the long haul, to set down roots and grow my little business into something special. Our paths were dividing under our feet, and she could feel it happening even in this triumphant moment.

It won't always be small, I thought. Give me a year. Two at the most. But I never said that out loud, and it's just as well that I didn't. Growing Turtle Island into something big was going to take a little more time than that.

20/20 HINDSIGHT:
Don't Pay Too Much for Money

One constant need for all businesses, bootstrapped or otherwise, it's the never-ending need for money to keep the business running. Some people look at me as some kind of business genius who started a company on $2,500 and grew it into the multimillion-dollar success that Tofurky has become. In fairness to those misguided people, that did happen. However, as you can see already, they're wrong about the genius part.

I worked super hard for a long time, but I didn't do this with $2,500 and incredible skills. I did this with $2,500 and my big brother, Bob, who rescued the business time after time with the money it needed to keep running. Especially in the lean, early years, Bob had a big heart and a fairly weak sense of things like risk. He quickly moved into the role of banker for Turtle Island, and he stayed there as my main funding source for more than a decade.

In the 1980s, the market for plant-based foods was just starting to emerge. Tempeh was confined to one small corner of that tiny marketplace. Banks were out there, and eventually we started borrowing from them, but it took many years for us to become a good risk for banks. Pioneers like me had few options for raising money other than friends and family. Venture capital wasn't really much of thing back then—and certainly not for natural foods businesses.

So thank goodness for Bob, and thank goodness for my mom, too, who put $5,000 of my "future inheritance" into Turtle Island. By relying on bank loans, family investment, reinvested profits, and other creative financing to grow Turtle Island, we've been able to keep the business family owned for almost forty years. That's given us the freedom to do things our own way, without anyone looking over our shoulders.

These days, venture capital *is* a thing, and natural foods bootstrappers are a hot commodity for equity investors—which honestly blows my mind. Lots of little start-ups are running on money secured by equity in the company. That's not a bad way to go, but be careful, bootstrapper. Taking on equity partners is taking on partners, and partners become bosses when they have more equity than you do.

My advice is that you don't pay any more than you have to for money. Go as far as you can on your own and with friends and family. Try to get to the point where you can expand beyond there with loans from banks or private lenders. If you do start paying for money by selling equity, try to stretch that money as far as it will go. That equity money comes with a price that makes it the most expensive money you will ever buy. Once you start down the path of selling equity, there's no turning back, but if you don't go very far down the path, you might be able to keep control of the business you're building.

COTTAGE INDUSTRY

I n which I insert moldy soybeans into the culture of the Washington Cascades, move from a tipi to a rodent-friendly travel trailer to an apartment I can afford on $300 a month, provide shelter for a troupe of piano-tuning clowns, and sell pallets of product to the Bhagwan Shree Rajneesh. Turtle Island Soy Dairy begins to keep records and hire actual employees, slowly transforming from an exciting possibility into an actual cottage industry that's worth at least $25,000 to someone who should know.

Bootstrappers, you understand how precarious this phase of growth appears to be. About once a week, something happens that makes you feel like everything is about to fall apart. But then it doesn't, right? Somehow, with long hours and creativity and the occasional nudge from a benevolent universe, you make it to the next week. That's the thread that runs through this chapter of my little business. But you know what? As poor as I was terms of in money, these were some of the richest years of my life.

Husum, Washington

The town of Husum, Washington, sits on the west side of rural Klickitat County in southern Washington along the Columbia River Gorge. The county is roughly the size of Rhode Island, but in 1982 it only had 25,000 residents and one stoplight. Actually, it still only has one stoplight. The crown jewel of the county is majestic Mount Adams, a 12,000-foot beauty whose glaciers feed the White Salmon and Klickitat rivers.

The White Salmon cuts through the middle of Husum with a ten-foot waterfall that gives the town a fresh, crisp, almost mystical ambiance. The river also marks the eastern edge of the wet, Douglas fir rainforests of the Washington Cascades and the western edge of the Ponderosa and oak lands to the east. Rattlesnakes are fairly common on the east side of the river, but they're almost never seen on the west side. Towering stands of timber, flower-studded meadows, deep rocky canyons, and lush farms make Klickitat County one of the most scenic counties in the United States.

Husum turned out to be a friendly little town, even toward "hippie-types" trying to make a living with soybeans. The town was an interesting mix of conservative alfalfa farmers and loggers, with a sprinkling of back-to-the-land, counterculture types. Husumites were all more or less just struggling to get by in this beautiful yet impoverished setting, so everyone seemed to get along pretty well. The whole town was excited to see new life breathed back into their little school.

The school had once been a center of activity in Husum, so our move-in caused quite a stir. One by one, all the neighbors stopped by to say hello and take a tour of the school that many of them had attended back in the day. They asked about what I was doing to the kitchen, pausing to give me an odd stare when I told them about how I was going to use the storage room as an incubator. They poked their heads into the classroom that I'd converted into an office and storage room, a room that many remembered as being the combined first- and second-grade classroom.

One person who dropped by was Luther, a 75-year-old who ran the town's water supply. Luther had a well on top of a hill overlooking the town, and he supplied water to all seventeen houses, the church, the café, the post office, the fire department, and the Department of Natural Resources compound. Now he would be selling water to my tempeh shop.

"How much will the water cost?" I asked him.

"Ten dollars a month," he said.

"I'm going to be using thousands of gallons. I don't think—"

"Ten dollars a month," he said, and he held firm on that price too, for the entire ten years we operated out of Husum.

I wanted the community to feel welcome in the building they had paid for with their taxes. Monday night soon became basketball night in the gym for anyone who was interested. On weekends, we showed movies. Whenever someone wanted to throw a town party—or wedding—I opened up the gym for that too, free of charge. No one seemed to mind the lack of heat in the cavernous halls of the building.

For my own housing, I first moved into to a funky rental house on a dirt road on the eastern, rattlesnake side of the White Salmon. To get there, it either took a twenty-minute drive up a rugged gravel road or a twenty-minute walk along a winding forest trail. Alex and I had planned to share the house on our own but then Belinda and Garry, and their two small girls, decided to move up to Husum as well. I made room for them by pitching my tipi outside the house and living there. All of us had either lived on or visited Stephen's Farm, so even though the living quarters were cramped, it felt pretty normal to us.

When the tempeh operation opened up in the spring of 1982, the local newspaper, White Salmon's *The Enterprise*, ran this front-page headline: "Tempeh Factory Opens in Husum." You know that times are hard when the opening of a tempeh shop grossing just over $1,000 per month is front-page news. The headline sent people running to the dictionary to find out what "tempeh" meant. It also lit up the phone at Tempeh Central, the little desk in my office/warehouse. I had calls from just about every out-of-work person in the valley, offering to be my secretary, maintenance technician, cook, or anything else they imagined was required by this supposedly prosperous modern factory. The trouble was that with so little money coming in, I could barely pay Alex and Belinda.

The first summer in Husum was challenging but magical. Alex had gone back to the Farm to visit his wife, Marian, and their two young kids. In June, he surprised me by showing up in Husum with his whole family. This struggling little tempeh business now had myself and two families to support. Alex and his family moved into a large tent outside the house that Belinda and her family lived in. To give them more space and also to prepare for the winter, I found a little rodent-friendly travel trailer for next to nothing and parked it out back of the school. That became my bedroom and den. For a kitchen, I cooked on a camp stove in one of the classrooms. My bathroom and shower was the spacious, unheated boys' restroom with its equally unheated water. It was a spartan life.

The entire staff of Turtle Island Soy Dairy was living on the cheap, but that was nothing new to any of us. For food, there was always tempeh and bags of soybeans, rice, and other grains to feast on. With a few added vegetables, fruits and other items, we were all doing just fine. This was a page right out of Stephen's playbook. "You can take care of yourself," he said, "and that is revolutionary too, because if you want independence, it comes from taking care of yourself."

Even working sixty hours and more every week, I had fun too. On basketball nights, we played until the sweat created a dangerously slick film on the gym's tile floor, making it dangerous to run on. Then we called it quits and headed up the road to the Logs Tavern in BZ Corner for pitchers of cheap Rainier Beer. In summer, the glacier-fed White Salmon River was perfect for a quick attitude-adjustment by jumping off the town's bridge into the cold waters—or floating down the frothy whitewater to Northwestern Lake. On Friday nights, I revived my mandolin playing

Seth and Alex Lyon pose out front of the old Husum School—the Turtle Island Soy Dairy, circa 1983. *(The Tofurky Company)*

and joined some other Husumites in forming the Sweaty Fingers Bluegrass Band. In these early days of the bootstrapping, with workloads so big and salary and benefits so small, keeping it light and fun as much as possible was a particularly important priority.

A Generous Landlord

In the fall of 1982, I had another moment of good fortune. I'd walked over to the post office to send out some mail. Bonnie, the Husum postmaster and entire post office staff, asked me if I might be interested in living in the one-bedroom apartment that she and her husband Dick had created on the second floor of their house.

"Definitely," I said. Their house was just across the bridge leading into town, a quick three-minute walk from the tempeh shop. I assumed it had hot water available for its shower too, which I was missing quite a lot by then. I also hoped that their apartment smelled better than the mouse urine and mold that gave my travel trailer its distinctive aroma.

"Great!" said Bonnie.

"The only problem, though, is that I'm a man of limited financial means."

"That's not a problem."

"I'm not sure I could afford the rent."

Bonnie smiled.

"Seth, we can't find anyone who can afford anything right now, the economy's so bad. We just thought it'd be good to have someone living there to keep it up until things get better. We'll let you stay there rent free."

To this day, I don't know what was behind her and Dick's unexpected generosity. Perhaps she was grateful for the way we let the community use the school without charging rent. Maybe she felt a mother's concern for this wayward child. Whatever the reason, Bonnie's offer was beautiful and timely for this young bootstrapper. I came to the end of my first year in Husum with a 13,000-square-foot school with a commercial kitchen for $150 per month and had a clean, roomy, heated apartment for zero dollars per month.

There's the idea out there that business is a mean, dog-eat-dog world. There may be some truth in that idea, but for me the generosity I'd found in Husum was deeply encouraging. It told me that business can also be a generous, people-helping-people world. Standing there in the post office, smiling at Bonnie like a happy idiot, I had a strong sense that the universe was letting me know that I was in the right place, doing the work I was meant to do, and doing it in the right way.

Building the Business

Building the business in Husum was a heady mixture of joy and terror. I was the president, production manager, production worker, chief financial officer, and janitor. I oversaw quality control, research and development, logistics, purchasing, sales, and marketing. As you might have already figured out, organization has never been my strong suit, so what I lacked in organization, I made up for with longer hours and regular apologies.

By then, Belinda was as good at making tempeh as I was. We still produced a few spoiled batches for the local bird population, but they were becoming less frequent as we continued to improve the temperature monitoring and overall plant cleanliness.

Our production days were Monday through Thursday. We set up 300 pounds of tempeh on Mondays and Wednesdays and harvested them on Tuesdays and Thursdays. I also handled most of the sales and delivery. On Mondays and Tuesdays, I was often on the road doing in-store demos in Eugene, Salem, Portland, and Seattle, or pitching our product line to new retailers. By 1983, we were up to five products—the original Soy Tempeh, Five Grain Tempeh, Tempehroni, Tempeh Burgers, and Barbeque Tempeh Burgers.

Nobody in Portland, not even our distributor, was willing to come to tiny little Husum to pick up our product, so that meant I had to trade in my trusty some-body-damage Datsun wagon for a more reliable Toyota pickup that had only minimal body damage but a lot of miles on it. Using scraps of plywood and Styrofoam, I built an insulated box to hold the product and slid that into the bed under the canopy.

Burger label, circa 1983. One of my many failed products. *(Seth Tibbott)*

Every Wednesday, I loaded the box with tempeh and delivered it myself to ten stores in Portland and a handful of Indonesians who knew me from those early days at the Java Restaurant. They were always amazed to see this American drive up with a load of their country's native food. After those direct deliveries, I took the rest to my distributor, Applegate, just sound of Portland. Then I'd crash on a couch at my friend Ken's house. If I had any leftover product, I'd sell it to him at a good price, and he would then sell it to his tempeh-loving friends.

Nobody was willing to deliver raw materials to Husum, so on Thursday morning, I broke down the insulated box in the back of the pickup and went shopping. I filled the back of the truck up

Early ad for Tempeh Burgers. (Jan Muir)

103

with bags of beans and grains, buckets of soy sauce, and all the boxes, plastic bags, and labels that we'd need to send product out the following week.

Fridays were reserved for taking orders. This was before the days of online orders. I didn't even have a fax machine or voice-mail, so all orders were taken over the phone. Imagine this: I'd sit by the phone and wait. When it rang, I'd pick up by the fourth ring, trying to sound casual, and take an order by asking the caller how much product they wanted for the coming week and then writing that order down in a notebook with a pencil. Hard to imagine, right? Those were my Fridays. Bathroom breaks were high-risk operations for me because we couldn't afford to miss an order.

Money was so tight in those days that it felt like any biggish mistake or largish new expense could bring the company down. The only way to cover operating expenses was by turning to my brother Bob to help pay for short-term items like more soybeans and long-term items like that Toyota pickup. His loans and my repayments became a revolving line of credit that was my sole source of credit until 1987, when I took out my first actual bank loan of $5,000.

Even though it felt like we were tiptoeing along the edge of failure, the business really was growing. Applegate got our products into stores beyond the Portland market. Their orders were nowhere near the thousand pounds per week that they had boasted, but they were still substantial. Other distributors signed on in Washington and Northern California. However, even as the top line grew by twenty percent each year, the bottom line was on a slightly downward trend. The more money we made, the more we seemed to lose. That was hard on everyone, and especially on Belinda and Alex, who were committed to the vision of the business but were not yet making a living wage.

Renting to Clowns

I needed to turn a profit, and by then I was less stupid enough as a businessman to know that there were two ways I could do it. One way was to sell more product. However, selling more product comes with increased expenses, so only a small part of that bigger top line would make it to the bottom line. The other way was to cut overhead. Every dollar I didn't spend on overhead would make it to the bottom line.

How was I going to do that, though? I was already overworking myself, paying myself next to nothing, and doing jobs that I should have hired others to do. I couldn't cut back on Belinda and Alex's small income flow. I couldn't cut back on supplies. But then I remembered that I *could* offset the rent cost by subletting the other three classrooms in the school. All I had to do was find businesses that could succeed anywhere—even in this backwater of American industry.

The first classroom was surprisingly easy to rent. Some good friends in Trout Lake—another pod of retired, wandering naturalists—had started a design business for museums and zoos and needed a good, open place to create their displays. It was a perfect fit. They were clean, quiet workers. They paid their hundred dollar rent on time. They were also good for a lunchtime game of H-O-R-S-E in the gym.

The second classroom went to a mom and pop business that made sturdy wooden gift boxes. Mom and Pop were a retired couple overflowing with kindness and good manners, and their boxes were beautifully made. They were just the right size for storing vinyl LPs, clothes, books—anything. You could fill these boxes with fruit and give them to people you didn't know well, and the people would actually be glad to get them because the boxes were so great. They were more like furniture than gift boxes.

However, Mom and Pop were about as bad at business as I had been when I first started, and they weren't getting any better. They charged $1.75 per box. No matter how much I tried to get them to raise the price, they charged $1.75 per box. When the price of wood went up, they charged $1.75 per box. Mom and Pop were thus always strapped for cash, going in and out of business, but all in all, they too were reliable rent-payers.

The third classroom sat empty for more than a year, but the two rented classrooms offset most of my own monthly rent, so I was feeling good enough as a landlord to not work too hard to find a third tenant. I had more or less given up on Classroom 3 when a big purple delivery truck drove into the parking lot of the school. I looked up from my desk. The truck had a large yellow umbrella on top. The umbrella was maybe five feet across, and it was wide open.

Two men got out of the truck, a bigger one and a smaller one, and started looking around as if they couldn't see the school they were standing in front of. I opened the front door of the school to see if I could help them locate the building. They both jumped back in mock terror and then smiled and came toward me.

"I'm Ace," said the bigger of the two, holding out his hand. He nodded toward the smaller man. "This here is Space."

I shook hands with both of them. Then they shook hands with each other. I could see now that clowns and pianos were painted on the side of the truck. You don't often see those two items painted on the same canvas.

"We're a traveling troupe of clowns" said Ace.

"But when the clowning is slow," said Space.

"Which is often," said Ace.

"We tune pianos," said Space.

"And we're looking for a place to make clown props," said Ace.

"And store them," said Space.

There's an unwritten rule for landlords—don't rent to clowns. However, when Ace handed me a crisp hundred-dollar bill, I did not hesitate. I shook his hand, shook Space's hand, watched them shake each other's hands, and became their landlord.

Three other adults and four kids piled out of the purple truck like it was a clown car—I suppose it was, technically—and moved right in to Classroom 3. They immediately set up their prop workshop. They'd invented a giant wooden wheel that the kids could sit inside of. They were soon taking turns pushing each other down the hallways of the school in these wheels. The classroom also became their living quarters, it turned out.

The clowns paid little more than that first hundred dollars, and they were high maintenance on top of that. Something always needed to be fixed. However, they were fun to be around. They brought a touch of Fellini to the tempeh operation. It was good to have them in the building just to keep us smiling as we struggled to make ends meet.

"A clown is very powerful," Ace once told me.

"A clown can say anything to anyone," said Space.

The clowns stayed about year and then moved on, looking for new people who needed laughs and also had out-of-tune pianos. That's a tough demographic. You have to go to them.

Rajneeshpuram

For 1983, Turtle Island had gross sales of just under $32,000, which was a healthy jump from the $21,000 we grossed in 1982. We were now selling more of our tempeh as refrigerated products, which had a 21-day shelf life and sat next to tofu in the faster-moving refrigerator section of stores. We also opened our own booth, Soyworld Café, across from the mainstage at the three-day-long Oregon Country Fair and introduced ourselves to hundreds of new customers there. Another boost came from a massive direct sale to the infamous Rajneeshpuram.

The big news in Oregon in the early 1980s was the arrival of the red-clad followers of Bhagwan Shree Rajneesh. The Rajneeshees purchased a 64,000-acre, overgrazed cattle ranch in Eastern Oregon to use as a commune and began to develop it into what was essentially a small city, Rajneeshpuram. Unlike the Farm in Tennessee, which had successfully reached out to their neighbors with respect and kindness, the Rajneeshees were combative from the start. The commune ignored Oregon's strict land use laws. It also moved many followers into the tiny, nearby city of Antelope so that they could take over the city council. They renamed the town "Rajneesh." It got worse from there. The silver lining, though, was that Rajneeshees liked tempeh.

In March of that year, two red-clad men from Rajneeshpuram—called *sannyasins*, or disciples—walked into the little café in Husum. The café was full of the usual coffee-drinking locals that morning, but when these two walked in, all coffee drinking and conversation stopped. The locals set down their cups and turned to stare.

"We're looking for Seth Tibbott," said the first of the sannyasins.

Betty, who ran the café with her husband Don, was behind the counter that morning. She nodded.

"Turtle Island Tempeh," said the other.

Betty lifted her pot of coffee and pointed in my direction.

"He's in the school there," she said, "across the bridge."

The sannyasins thanked her politely and took their leave. The door hadn't even closed when the gossip shock waves hit town and began spreading through the county. I suppose it's true that there's no such thing as bad publicity, but the strange looks I got from others did make me feel awkward around town for the next few weeks.

Over time, the leaders of the Rajneeshees revealed themselves to have a notable collection of pretty serious character flaws, but on that morning in March, the two guys who walked across the bridge to the school were down to earth and respectful. They greeted me politely and then explained their situation.

Their community was planning to host a celebration to honor their master, the Bhagwan Shree Rajneesh. They expected that ten thousand people from all over the world would be there. Because they were all vegetarians, they were interested in obtaining two thousand pounds of our Five Grain Tempeh for a big stir-fry meal during the celebration. That by itself would equal almost a month's worth of current sales.

"Sounds good to me," I told them.

It was a stretch to double production in June, but we managed to do it. Toward the end of the month I loaded up the Toyota with the first installment of the Rajneesh five-grain tempeh. The tempeh was frozen and packed in large corrugated boxes that weighed twenty-five pounds each. It was a hundred-mile drive from Husum to Rajneeshpuram, mostly on two-lane, sagebrush-lined roads. I rolled the windows down to let the sweet smell of juniper and sage fill the cab.

Around noon, I stopped in the small town of Antelope, population sixty, which was about ten miles from Rajneeshpuram. The town would not be renamed Rajneesh for another year, but the presence of the commune was noticeable. Dozens of red-clad sannyasins walked along the road carrying flowers past the tiny post office, weather-beaten houses, and deserted store buildings. My old friend and former college roommate, Tim, was with me for this delivery. We stopped for lunch at a small, Rajneesh-run store and café. Inside was a display case with vegetarian food. To one side of the building was what looked like a typical, small-town convenience store. However, this store offered expensive European cigarettes, high-end chocolates, and shelves of imported wine.

We bought lunch and some cold drinks and then got back into the truck for another five miles on blacktop and then more miles on gravel roads after that. Finally, we stopped at the entrance gate and a team of Rajneesh security guards. We didn't see any guns, but we got a lot of scowls from the security team. We told the team that we were here to deliver some tempeh for the world celebration.

The sannyasin who stood at the window eyed us closely. Then he called in on his radio and waited. Standing on boulders looking down at us with folded arms, a handful of others gave us the same general attitude of skepticism and dislike. Our guy got a call back on the radio. He stepped away from us and conferred quietly over the radio. Then he came back to the window of the truck, gave us another once-over, and waved us forward.

The road from the outer gate to the center of the commune was a long, bumpy gravel road down a valley toward the John Day River. We passed a new reservoir lined with young trees and new grass. The commune was already repairing much of the environmental damage that came from generations of overgrazing in this valley. At the bottom of the valley, the land flattened out. It was covered by a mixture of permanent structures and hundreds of tents, all of them pitched in neat, long rows for the thousands of guests who were soon to arrive. The streets were filled with thirty-something, mostly white people who were wearing many shades of red and who seemed to radiate enthusiasm and happiness.

We passed the commune's large "city hall" building. A woman came out and directed us to the kitchen, which turned out to be an enormous canvas tent with a dozen refrigerator and freezer semi-trailers parked alongside it. At the kitchen, the sannyasins

Perhaps the biggest tempeh feast ever in the USA. Ten thousand "sannyasin" followers of the Bhagwan Shree Rajneesh from all over the world dined on Turtle Island Five Grain Tempeh Stir Fry on July 6, 1983, at Rajneeshpuram, near Antelope, Oregon. *(Jim Wells)*

who'd made the order came up to us and greeted us warmly. Suddenly, instead of being on a mysterious journey into the heart of this commune, it was just another tempeh delivery.

I made two more deliveries before the celebration and then, in July, I was on hand to observe the cooking of what I believe may still be the largest tempeh meal ever cooked—at least in the US. The Rajneesh chefs cubed the tempeh and then cooked it on twenty commercial woks with propane burners. They served the tempeh over rice and added veggies and a sweet and sour sauce. It was delicious.

After the meal, I followed the sannyasins up a dirt road and joined them in forming long lines on either side of the road. Soon the sannyasins around me burst into an excited frenzy as a grey Rolls-Royce appeared in the distance. The car moved very slowly down the road, stirring little dust. When the Rolls passed me, the sannyasins beside me cried out with joy and lofted flowers onto the car's hood. The Bhagwan Shree Rajneesh himself was behind the wheel, taking his daily drive in one of the ninety-three Rolls-Royces he owned. He had a slight, wry smile, a long, white beard, and glazed eyes that wandered briefly from the road to his adoring followers. After he passed, the two women beside me hugged and told each other that the Bhagwan had definitely looked at them.

I made several more deliveries to Rajneeshpuram after the festival—including a flight into their private airport with my friend Bill, the boot repairer, who had by then gotten his pilot's license. As bad as the commune turned out to be for Wasco County, it was certainly good for business. Two months after the festival, the kitchen, trailers, and woks were gone, replaced by a field of young wheat starting to make its way up from the finely tilled soil.

By the fall of 1984, the commune's leadership had spun out of control. Rajneeshees were implicated in poisoning 751 people in

The Dalles, the Wasco County seat, with salmonella. Later, even more devious plots came to light, including the attempted murder of several Oregon politicians. We never sold any more tempeh to the Rajneeshees after the salmonella poisoning. In 1985, the Bhagwan was arrested at the airport in Charlotte, North Carolina, trying to flee the country. The commune itself fell apart not long after that. They were done with their international community in Oregon.

However, I was not quite done with them. That fall, I won $50 and the coveted first prize at the Trout Lake Tavern Halloween Costume Contest by dressing as the Bhagwan in jail. I put on a long blue robe and danced inside one of my six-foot-tall tempeh rolling racks that I labeled "Charlotte Jail."

Bookkeeping

Turtle Island's gross sales rose to $45,000 in 1984, which was great, but it wasn't enough to keep Belinda and Alex on staff. My friends and fellow pie-in-the-sky dreamers decided they needed to find a better way to feed their families. That was a tough loss for the business and for me personally. These were my comrades, the two people who'd really bought into the dream of where this thing could go and had invested not just their time but themselves to make that happen. It frustrated me that the business hadn't grown fast enough to pay them better and offer bigger rewards for investing so much in this dream of mine.

But there was no time to wallow in feelings of sadness or regret. Turtle Island may have grown slowly, but there was no way to roll it back to a one-man shop. I had too many orders to fill— and a big brother to repay. So I had to hire replacements quickly, and this time I had to pay them with actual paychecks, not as contractors, which meant withholding taxes and doing all the other things about payroll that I didn't understand. That made the whole operation feel more real than surreal—even with the piano-tuning clowns roaming the halls. However, I was still mostly a tempeh maker, not a number cruncher, and I knew I needed help.

Enter Rosie, who kept the books for several other businesses in Klickitat County. From our first meeting, it was clear that she knew her stuff. She was quick to laugh too, which helped me to overcome my dread of bookkeeping. Every week, she came to see me in my little classroom/office/warehouse to record sales, pay the bills, and do all the rest that went with it.

One week, Rosie sat me down after she'd done the numbers.

"Seth," she said. "I think you should get a computer."

"I have a computer," I said, pointing to my head. This was 1984, remember. People weren't wearing computers on their wrists in those days.

"Oh Lord," she said. "You need something that works better than *that*."

She threw her head back and laughed, but then just as quickly, she stopped laughing and looked me in the eye.

"I'm dead serious," she said. She then explained in some detail how a computer would add everything up for me, keep a running total of sales and expenses, and help me to run my business as if it were an actual business.

"Especially when you're this size," she said, using her forefinger and thumb to show me the universal sign for teeny tiny, "keeping track of your numbers up to the minute is the difference between making it and not making it."

Rosie had a point. I could see that. But I remained skeptical. The only computer I'd ever spent any time with was the Commodore 64 that my friend Charlie used to keep track of his household budget and play Pong. I didn't really have a household budget to keep track of, and at the moment, I was working seventy- and eighty-hour weeks. I didn't really have any time to play Pong, although that would have been cool because Pong was *amazing*.

The compromise we reached was for Rosie to come to Husum once a week, gather all the information she needed, and then go home and use her own computer to process it. After that, she printed out monthly income statements for the business and tracked the employee deductions and net pay.

The Local Labor Pool

The labor pool in Husum was small but colorful. For the most part, only women applied for the production work. Most of them were the wives of the loggers and contractors who were just getting by during that recession. With the economy in such bad shape, they were happy to have the income. However, because I was offering the lowest wages allowed by law, they also tended to move on as soon as something better came along—or they ran off with someone—or had to work a few things out at the county jail.

Rosie the Bookkeeper worked on contract, so my first actual hire was Joe the Maintenance Guy, who came in every Sunday night to sweep and mop the hallways, clean the bathrooms, and tidy up the office. Then I hired two local women to work part-time making tempeh. They each worked about thirty hours a week, and I backed off my eighty-hour weeks to a more manageable fifty or sixty hours.

"Mindy" was one early production worker, a young, religious Husum woman. She had the sneaky habit of changing the radio to James Dobson's socially conservative *Focus on the Family* whenever I left the kitchen. She also had a habit of getting into relationships that ended badly, including a marriage that used our gym as its wedding venue. Born and raised in Husum, she had a soft voice and great attitude on life.

"Amber" was another early and enduring production worker. She and her two daughters lived a mile and half from town in the basement of a house that she was building all on her own. She paid for wood and other materials with cash as she had it, so it was a slow process. When she came to work for Turtle Island, she had finished her house up to the first floor—the floor of the first floor, that is. She put a heavy tarp over that and moved her little family from a converted school bus into the daylight basement. Over the next two years, she framed up the rest of the house while living in the basement.

Amber was relentless with that project and just about everything else. While that kind of single-mindedness sometimes got on people's nerves, it was great for the tempeh shop. She was efficient in the kitchen, a hard worker, and completely capable of running the production line by herself when I was gone. She trained herself to do demos at trade shows and in natural foods stores. She even loaned the business some money during one of our many cash-flow bottlenecks. As you'll soon see, she eventually became my landlord, which made for an interesting checks-and-balances relationship.

One of my favorite local employees was a big-boned Swedish woman who lasted for several years. "Ingrid" had a wry sense of humor that made her fun to work with, but she also led a tough life there in the valley. She'd been married and divorced several times, and had ended upin the hills outside of Husum, a place that was kind of like the Alaska of Klickitat County. People went there to be left alone.

One day Ingrid told me that she needed a week off from tempeh making so she could go into Portland to get a nose job. I thought her nose looked fine—in fact, it looked a lot like mine. But I had no problem giving her the time off; so two weeks later, off she went. That might have been the end of the story, aside for her coming back to make tempeh with Julia Roberts' nose on her face. However, while she was away, her place got busted for running a meth lab. According to Ingrid, the other people living there used her absence as an excuse to set it up.

It was a big story for a small valley, and it spread at the speed of gossip, which is only slightly slower than the speed of light. Not surprisingly, traveling at that speed skewed some of the details of the story. My neighbor Dave came in a couple days later and told me about a conversation he'd overheard at the café.

"I knew there was something fishy going on at that school building," said one woman to her friends. "They had to be making something more than *moldy soybeans*."

Her friends all clucked in agreement.

"The moldy soybeans are just a front," said another.

"I'll bet you're right," said a third woman. "I'll bet those hippie-types are the ones who set up the lab in Ingrid's trailer house."

Dave interrupted the conversation at that point and tried to set them straight, but sometimes the story is better than the facts. In the end, Ingrid was able to get her home back, and because of her humor and persistence, she gradually managed to get her story into the collective consciousness of Husum, but it was a long time before the suspicions about Turtle Island died down.

I could go on and on with the many local employees who came and went, but I'll end with "Cindy," who was one of the poorest women in town and partnered to an unemployed alcoholic. They had no car—or visible means of support—so I had to assume they were both living off the lousy tempeh wages she brought home. It didn't seem like a happy situation. She came in more than once with a frozen expression that didn't soften for hours.

One day she also came in flat-out drunk. A thick smell of alcohol followed her like a cloud of exhaust, which I suppose it was. I quickly considered my options. Firing her was one of them, and this was a good reason for it. She could barely stand up. Who knew what damage she might do to the tempeh? Then again, the wage scale hadn't risen at all over the years, and I had already seen most of the Husum labor pool come and go. People weren't exactly lining up for the next opening to wear out their backs making tempeh for minimum wage. Business aside, I had to wonder what would happen if she went home without a job. I didn't have any proof of abuse going on there, but I had a suspicion. I didn't want to make a bad thing worse.

"Cindy," I said.

She gave me a big fake smile, like nothing was wrong.

"Why don't you go back home?"

Her smile dropped away at "go," and her eyes dropped down at "home."

"Please sober up," I told her. "I'll cover your shifts."

She nodded.

"Come back in three days, and then we'll talk about your job."

That's what she did too. She came back and apologized and promised to never do that again. She was true to her word too, for the next two months or so.

The First Big-Money Offer

Turtle Island grossed $59,000 in 1985, which was another nice jump for the top line. Given all the new expenses with payroll, however, it had no impact on my $300 monthly salary. I wasn't getting rich, but I was still having fun figuring things out. I was making my loan payments to Bob, mostly on time. I was the leading employer in Husum. Things were okay.

And then one day, out of the blue, I got a call from a tofu maker in Seattle. He said he'd gotten a large investment of venture capital—whatever that was—and was planning to build a new plant that would make him the largest tofu and tempeh brand in the US. Okay, I thought. Good for you. Then he told me how much he liked Turtle Island Tempeh products. Okay, I thought. Then he asked me a question that hit me in the gut.

"Would you be interested in selling the company?"

I don't remember what I actually muttered in response, but I guess it was neutral enough for him to continue. These were the details:

First, there'd be a lump sum buyout of $25,000.

"Wait," I said. "What?"

I'd heard correctly. Twenty-five thousand dollars. I could pay off all my loans and still have more left over than I'd taken home since starting the business. But what I couldn't believe was that someone thought my business was worth that much money. He said he'd bring me up to work for him in Seattle for my dream salary of $1,000 a month. Turtle Island would continue as a brand in the northwest. The national brand would then sell our tempeh under their label in a slick vacuum-packed box with a sauce packet.

"It's tempting," I said. "It's really tempting."

Twenty-five thousand dollars! It made me step back from what I was doing and see for the first time that my dream had turned into an actual business—a cottage industry that was worth something to more than just me. I flashed back to that afternoon in 1981 when I raised my hand for Mr. Businessman at the Small Business Administration seminar. Look at this, I told him in my brain. My dream is a real small business.

I wanted to say yes—or at least a large part of me wanted to. The thing that hung me up was the idea of my beautiful tempeh selling under someone else's brand. Finally, after seven months of looking into the offer and considering my options, the guy in Seattle told me he needed an answer. Was I going to sell and come work for him or not?

That's when it hit me how much I loved this little business. I loved it with a kind of parental love, and I couldn't just sell this kid that I'd been raising for the last five years, even if it wasn't living up to expectations. I wasn't ready to give up on the dream. I didn't really want to work for anyone else, either. It was a huge relief to finally call him back and turn down the big money.

Was I still in the bootstrap game? Yes, I was. Turtle Island might have been a disorganized, directionless, and not-particularly-profitable albatross hung around my neck, but at least it was *my* disorganized, directionless, and not-particularly-profitable albatross.

20/20 HINDSIGHT:
Fire Yourself Regularly

I was never very good at firing people. In the thirty-four years that I ran the company, I only "let go" of a handful of people. Partly this was due to the small labor pool in the area. Firing someone meant having to find someone else to replace them, and with the wages I was paying—especially in these early days—that wasn't ever easy. I was also reluctant to fire people because it felt like I was just passing the problem on to some other business. If I didn't try to help them improve as employees, then they were just going to keep getting fired in the future.

The one employee I fired over and over was me. In these early chapters of my business life, I couldn't afford to fire myself because I didn't have enough money to hire a replacement. I had to do all the jobs. Even when I did start to hire others for production, I had to keep working production too. And it's likely going to be the same for you too, bootstrapper, as you get your business launched.

However, as the company grows, it's important to start firing yourself from the jobs that others can do better than you or that take you away from more important work. Firing myself from the job of keeping the books was a great decision. I was a lousy bookkeeper, and Rosie was great at it. She did the job better than I would have ever done it, even if I'd had the time to train myself to do it right.

That's more or less what happened every time I fired myself. When I fired myself as business manager and hired my friend Dave, he ran the business *way* more efficiently than I ever did. When I fired myself and hired our first sales manager, Mark, sales really ramped up. Sales are the life blood of the company, so I should have done this sooner. I paid Mark more than I paid myself for many years, but it was worth it.

Was I lousy at all these jobs I got fired from? With some of them, maybe a little. But the bigger problem was that I was working too many jobs at once. I couldn't give any one or two jobs the time and care they required. The more jobs I got fired from, the better work I did with the jobs I kept.

When you do fire yourself from one of your bootstrapping jobs, make sure you give your replacement the power to do that job *better*. You hired them because they have a better skillset for the job than you do, so don't hold them back by overmanaging them. The new hire will probably find a more effective way of doing the job, so don't have hurt feelings when that happens. You *want* that to happen. That's why you fired yourself in the first place.

THE ITCH

I n which running a business becomes not as much fun as it used to be when I was working even longer hours, racing from one headache to another, which leads me to look elsewhere for creative outlets—renting four local trees as my new home, traveling, working on a book, and teaching TV camera crews how to make fifteen quiet hippie-types look like an angry mob of eco-warriors. Through it all, Turtle Island continues to grow no matter how many mistakes I make, which means outgrowing the Husum School, which was also not as much fun anymore.

Bootstrappers, if you haven't gotten there already, I'm here to tell you that there comes a point when the long-term dream turns into a real-life business that is just not as cool as the dream. What do you do then? Do you just keep grinding away at it? Do you change things up? Do you link arms in front of angry log trucks? For me, the answer was to start looking for a way out, and happily, I failed at that just like I'd failed at everything else.

Treehouse

By 1984, the economy was finally starting to pick up again, even in Klickitat County. It wasn't long before Bonnie and Dick had a *paying* renter for their cozy apartment, and I had to look for accommodations elsewhere. My friend and employee Amber came to the rescue by offering me the use of her five-acre meadow for my tipi. I jumped at her offer and moved back into the tipi for the rest of spring and summer.

It was great to be back in the tipi. There's nothing better than tipi life in the late spring and summer and early fall. However, there's nothing worse than tipi life during the brutal winters of the Washington Cascades, so even as I sipped my herbal tea—or whatever—and tended the evening fire that June, my mind was already racing ahead to figure out better housing for the winter.

I found the answer on a visit to another former wandering naturalist, Kirk, who'd built a seasonal home about twelve feet off the ground between two big fir trees and a cedar. It reminded me of the tiny houses that my Grandpa Seth built as a private retreat on his property in Minnesota—before tiny houses were a thing. With a cedar shake roof and siding, Kirk's treehouse looked like a giant nest. I could imagine some kind of Hobbit-like creature living in there. There was even a counterweighted drawbridge "to keep the riffraff out."

Inspired by Kirk's treehouse, I scouted out four good-sized fir trees not far from Amber's house-in-progress. They were close together and large enough that I thought they'd be able to support a treehouse. When I brought the idea up with her, she didn't hesitate.

"Sure," she said. "How about twenty-five dollars a month?"

That was in my price range.

We drew up a treehouse manifesto to seal the deal. In short, the treehouse was all on me to build, along with an outhouse, and when I moved out, it all belonged to Amber. Amber reserved the right to veto whoever else lived there "if there is reasonable cause for alarm." My rent included water, a 20-amp circuit to use as I thought best, and an extension to her home phone. It was perfect. I figured that if I could live there for two years and spend fifteen hundred dollars or less on the treehouse, I'd be way ahead of what I would have spent on rent anywhere else in Klickitat County.

Amber and I signed our agreement in July, and I immediately went to work gathering the tools and materials I thought I would need. I wasn't much of a carpenter, but I had spent some hours under my dad's tutelage learning the basics of hand and power tools. That gave me the confidence I needed to start pulling together a pile of new and recycled wood that would later become the treehouse I would somehow design and build.

You might be wondering about how I planned to build a treehouse while simultaneously running my cottage-industrial tempeh shop. The answer is obvious enough for the careful readers of this book—Plan? What's a plan? I just decided to do it because I didn't want to be in a tipi in November. However, it's worth noting that by then, Turtle Island ran itself fairly well. I had failed so regularly and broadly that my mistakes had taught me most of what I needed to know to run a productive tempeh shop. I also had a seasoned production crew that knew how to make tempeh without me, so the business no longer required the same amount of time and problem-solving as it did in the early days.

So I turned to treehouse, and as soon as the word got out that I was building a treehouse, kind and curious people came by to help turn another of my unrealistic ideas into a surprisingly cool reality. A neighbor of Amber's donated six big Douglas fir poles and drew up plans for how to connect them to my rental trees about fifteen feet off the ground. The poles would become the beams that connected the trees and held up the house. It took me forever to drill through the poles and trees to get my foundation in place, but once that was done, the work sped up.

As a side note, a lot of people think that it damages a tree to drill a hole all the way through it. They believe that wrapping beams to a tree with rope or cable would be better for the tree, but nothing could be further from the truth. Cables can actually girdle the vital, living cambium of the tree, and kill it. Drilled holes are less of a problem than woodpeckers are. The holes I drilled almost forty years ago were filled with one-inch threaded rods and pine tar, and the trees remain healthy and happy to this day.

On top of these beams, I laid out two-by-eight joists and nailed three-quarter-inch plywood on top of that. With a floor to walk on, framing up the rest of the walls was a lot easier—for my friend, Bill, and others who came by to help. I cantilevered a deck out on three sides of the house and ran wooden stairs down to the ground from the back of one deck. It was late August by the time all the walls were up, and the deck was finished. I was still putting in my time at the tempeh shop, but my imagination was up in the trees.

By September, I had plywood nailed to all the walls and rafters. I covered it with tarpaper to protect it from the weather. That would be my siding and roofing for the first year. The next step was to insulate everything with fiberglass insulation so that even if winter came early, I could stay warm in an insulated box. Fortunately, though, winter held off all through September and into October. I dug a trench to Amber's house-in-progress and ran water, power, and a phone line from her place to the treehouse.

Next, I hit the second-hand building supply stores in Portland for cool-looking windows, three of which contained stained glass. Brother Bob shipped out an old Dutch door from a small cottage that my dad had built on the Chesapeake in 1920. I was glad to have those in place before the rains set in. Then I decided to stretch the budget to get a small but efficient Jotul wood stove.

The treehouse I built in four trees, out of mostly scavenged lumber, and which I rented for $25 per month, near Husum, Washington. *(Sue Tibbott)*

I moved into my snug, barely finished winter home on October 15, 1984. The main floor was eleven by sixteen feet wide with an open floorplan. Coming into the Dutch door from the front deck, you entered the living room half of the main floor. On the floor was an old rug salvaged from Grandpa Seth's tiny house. The south wall had a floor-to-ceiling bookcase and a fold-down desk. A rotary dial telephone—maybe you've seen a picture of one—hung from the wall. To the north of the door was a six-foot window seat that folded out to become a small bed capable of sleeping two friendly people. Lying on the bed, you could look out a large picture window onto the bird feeders on the deck or up to the stars though a large skylight.

Behind the living area, the other half of the main floor contained my kitchen. The Jotul wood stove sat on a brick hearth in the right corner. Next to it was the kitchen counter, complete with a sink plumbed with cold running water, a three-burner stove salvaged from the mouse-habitat trailer, and an under-counter fridge. There was plenty of counter space, and two scavenged cabinets provided more than enough storage. Over the winter, I built a silverware drawer with a twisted wooden handle and installed track lights above the counter. I even added a little cat door for Shakespeare the Cat, who used the whole treehouse as the ultimate kitty gym.

Above the back half of the main floor, I added a sleeping loft that I climbed up to with the help of a small ladder. For a bed, I bought a four-inch slab of foam rubber. For a dresser, I stacked up a half-dozen of those mom-and-pop gift boxes from my renters. I had a small wooden casement window at the back of the loft. For several months, that window was on the route of a flying squirrel who liked to swoop onto the back wall of the treehouse at two in the morning to check on me through that window. Everything okay? he seemed to ask. It is, I thought. He seemed to be okay with having me in his neighborhood after dark.

After the first year in the house, I added a four-by-eight-foot cupola. It could be accessed via a set of narrow steps chiseled into a peeled log and then through a trap door. This was the highest point of the treehouse, about thirty feet above the ground. From its windows, there was a great view of the valley below and the hills beyond. Its foldout bench was always a cheery place to settle in with a mug of herbal tea and a good book.

When it came time to relieve myself—I know you're wondering this—I walked out to the small "treehouse peehouse" that I'd connected to one side of the deck. It was like any other outhouse except that it came with a long metal stove pipe that dropped down fifteen feet to a large covered hole in the ground. My friend Jan etched a whale onto a narrow glass window and gave that to me for the back wall of the treehouse peehouse.

The treehouse was a great place to live for many reasons beyond its affordable rent. One was that it was located on a Frisbee-golf course that friends had carved out of Amber's and another neighbor's land. The holes were just wooden poles instead of the baskets with chains that you see today, but we each adopted one of the nine holes and tried to outdo each other creating tee boxes and obstacles that made the course a challenge. I played at least nine holes with someone most nights after work, usually accompanied by Shakespeare the Cat.

In the end, I rented those four trees for a lot longer than two years. I lived in the trees into the 1990s—for the rest of my life as a bachelor and the rest of my time in Husum.

The School

Another factor that made me itch for something new was our situation at the grade school. In the spring of 1986, I found out the school board had fielded an offer on the school. The prospective buyer was a local businessman—I'll call him "Shady." He had supposedly come up to Husum from some big city, and it hadn't taken long for everyone in the White Salmon valley to become leery of him. But he'd made an offer of $60,000, and the new school superintendent was determined to finally sell this useless school of theirs.

I had the right to match the offer, but I only had one month to come up with the money, and I had no idea how I could ever get my hands on that kind of capital, or if I'd even want to spend it on the school if I could. Turtle Island grossed $67,000 in 1986, another modest increase from the year before, but between having to purchase more supplies and hire more employees, there wasn't any money left over. I was *still* living on $300 a month.

Meanwhile, Shady came by the tempeh shop talking all kinds of garbage. He was going to start a health club and offered to let me and a friend run it. The rent was never going to change. Everything was going to be cool. But I knew it was going to be *so* not cool.

"I'm hocking my ass on this school," he told me, "because this place is going to go wild, and when it does, I'm going make some serious money. Because I need it."

I looked pretty seriously at buying the building out from under Shady, but the tempeh shop was already starting to show signs of outgrowing the school. As production increased, we needed more water, and we disposed of more water. With a small town of seventeen houses all pulling water from the same well, the tempeh shop was starting to become a water hog that affected water pressure for everyone else. One time a neighbor called to ask if we could hold off washing down our equipment so she could take a shower.

The school's outdated septic system wasn't exactly designed to serve an expanding soybean operation. In spite of our efforts to prevent beans from slipping past the floor drains, a lot of beans found their way to the septic tank—so many that pumping the tank became an annual event, kind of like the swallows returning to Capistrano, but with soybeans. And there was no natural gas, just the more expensive propane. And the roof leaked. And this was Husum still, the little town that no one wanted to deliver to or ship from.

Was I willing to not just buy the school but then invest even more to make sure it could handle expanded production? I still loved the old school and still dreamed of seeing it become the hub not just for Husum, but for a growing environmental community in the valley. In the end, though, I just couldn't do it. It was too big of a risk. At the end of the month, I called the superintendent and told him as much.

The next day, a big delivery truck backed up to the school and unloaded pallet after pallet of windows and building supplies into the gym. The ownership of those materials would later become a matter of some debate. In the present moment, however, they meant the end of community basketball. The next week, Shady doubled my rent. It was still a good deal, but I could tell the best days in the Husum school were behind me.

A Role Model

Also in 1986, I tried to stay engaged creatively by making my first trip to the natural food industry's biggest trade show, Expo West, in the Anaheim Convention Center right across the street from Disneyland. I wasn't an exhibitor yet. I went mostly to meet up with sales brokers, distributors, and buyers for store chains so that Turtle Island could expand its distribution. However, no one was interested in talking to me—no one. Turtle Island was too small to attract interest from brokers, who wanted at least $5,000 per month in commissions. Most of our tempeh products didn't have a long enough shelf life for long-range distribution, either.

So instead of making great deals to expand our market, I walked the floor and checked out the hundreds of booths that were exhibiting their products. Most of the booths were uninspiring. However, I did meet one person who intrigued me, Al Jacobson. He had on a wild chef hat embroidered with the words "The Wizard of Foods," and he wrapped a rainbow-colored scarf around his neck. He paced back and forth in front of his booth for The Garden of Eatin'. He was a short, spry man who was well into his sixties, and he never stopped moving. He was one of a kind at Expo West, a loud, colorful counterpoint to all the rest of the serious business-types in the exhibit hall.

I parked myself at his booth for the next two hours. Al was so obviously excited about natural food—and *life*. I couldn't believe how refreshing it was, and then it made me scratch my head. Why was he so different from all the other businesspeople there? Most of them wore suits and ties and spoke in sensible, measured tones about the blah blah qualities of their blah blah products.

The prevailing thought was that when you had a new product to market, you should show it in a familiar, "professional" manner. Not so for the Wizard of Foods. He bounced around as he talked. He laughed with real joy. I thought, everyone here should be as excited about natural foods and life as the Wizard of Foods.

Al told me in an excited whisper that'd he just bought twenty tons of blue corn and was going to make it into tortilla chips, which at that time were all yellow.

"But how do you think people will go for that?" I asked.

He laughed. But then he studied me more seriously. He stepped closer to me and confided something that has stayed with me ever since.

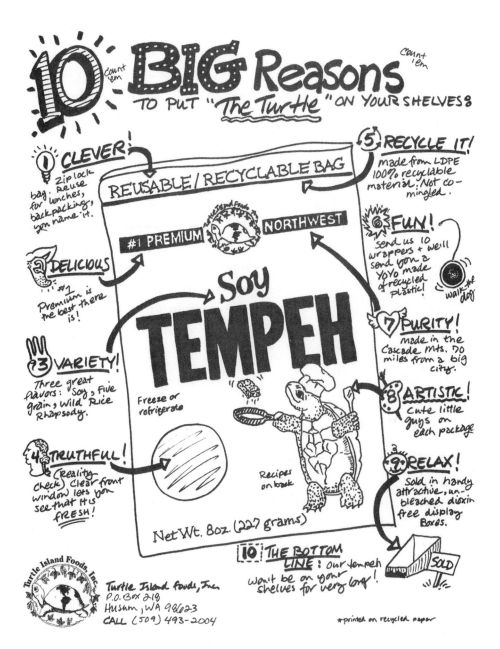

In 1987, we introduced our tempeh in recyclable Ziploc bags. When customers sent in ten bags, we recycled them into yo-yos, and later frisbees, which we sent back to customers. *(Marcia Barrentine)*

"Sometimes," he said, "you just know."

Before I left his booth, the Wizard invited me to stop by and see him whenever I was in town. The next time I saw him was just a year later, and in that time, his blue corn chips had become a huge hit. He'd sold a million dollars' worth of blue corn chips at one specialty foods chain alone.

"They thought I was crazy!" he told me, laughing. "Nobody thought I'd sell a single bag."

I congratulated him, and sincerely too. I wasn't envious of his success at all. But looking back, I can see now that I was a little envious of *him*. What I saw in him—the energy and imagination and just plain magic—was what I wanted to see in myself. I was tired of trying to be the kind of businessman that others expected me to be. It seemed to me that part of my itch to do something new came from the cognitive dissonance created by trying to be something I wasn't.

The Treehouse Book

As the 1980s wore on, the business kept growing in spite of my growing discontent. Our gross sales for 1987 were $73,000. In 1988, we hit $86,000 and added several new positions, including hiring my friend Dave as a business manager.

Dave was a great addition to the team. In his mid-thirties, he was not afraid of hard work. He was smart and organized in a way that I was not. That made him the perfect counterpoint to my rambling ideas. He thought in terms of flow charts and spreadsheets, which soon meant bringing the first computer into the business—and Husum. All of this advancement was great. I even gave myself a little bump in salary. However, the more Turtle Island evolved into a normal business, the less it felt like my own creative expression and the more I felt that itch for something new.

One way I tried to scratch that itch was with writing. My dad had been a romantic—a poet, storyteller, and artist—who ended up living a work life of quiet desperation, grinding away at a job for the federal government in Washington, D.C. He was a lively man of great creativity who told wonderful stories, often through his penguin drawings. He always encouraged me to be a writer or to get into some other kind of creative work that would be soul-satisfying. So I thought I'd give it a shot.

I started by writing little stories for *The Sun*, which is still one of my favorite magazines of all time. My favorite was a few paragraphs about living in the trees, and I followed that with another story that was published in the *Whole Earth Review*. The response was amazing. I got all kinds of cards and letters from others who had moved into the trees, some with invitations to visit.

This got me thinking. There was a popular coffee-table book out called *Handmade Houses: A Guide to the Woodbutcher's Art*, which featured creative, owner-built homes, but there was nothing in it about the "woodbutchers" like me who had taken their craft to the trees. Why not write a book on these treehouses I was learning about? It seemed easy enough. It also seemed like just the right creative project to keep my imagination alive. I mentioned the idea to a few friends, and they all agreed that it would be a hit.

I began to imagine that this project could change things for me. Instead of being a failing businessman, I could become a famous author. This new creative dream fit perfectly with my idealistic, romantic self. I could feel that this was going to be big.

Teaming up with my friend Laura, a talented photographer, we began to visit, photograph, and write about the tree dwellers who'd written to me. I started to leave the running of the tempeh shop in the hands of Dave and my other employees for days and weeks at a time. In Cocoa Beach, Florida, we photographed the treehouse of a newspaper magnate. His one-room treehouse had a thatched roof and an old manual typewriter that he used to write his editorials while overlooking the Atlantic Ocean. We found a sprawling $100,000 treehouse in central Florida spread through a large oak tree, complete with Belgian cut glass and hardwood floors. There was the guy who built his treehouse in suburban Minneapolis and then fought City Hall—and won—after they demanded that he tear it down.

Treehouse in Florida that cost over $100,000 with Belgian glass and hardwood floors, in 1989. (John Moran)

The most famous or infamous treehouse we found was a massive treehouse in a large stand of Douglas Fir trees near Olympia, Washington. Since it was relatively close, we went back several times to photograph it. Every time we visited, the owner had something new to show us—a new floor, a stainless-steel refrigerator, a high-end stereo. We never saw him work or talk about work, so we assumed he was either a trust-funder or a drug dealer. But we were wrong. One morning I opened the paper and found out that he was a bank robber who'd been shot by the police after a job went bad. Before that, he had robbed more than forty banks in the Seattle area, always retreating back to the trees until the trail grew cold and the money grew thin.

The more I strayed from tempeh to work on the book, the more I envisioned its success. The only bit of weirdness that made me wonder about this path was a comment I heard more than once. When I contacted my fellow tree dwellers to ask about a visit, a lot of them said something like, "Sure. Come on by. But you know, some other guy came by last week. He said he was writing a treehouse book too." It didn't bother me, though, that someone else was out there working on a book. On the contrary, it confirmed that this was a path worth following. I just had to make a push on my traveling and writing so I could get to market first.

Spotted Owls and Bulldozers

Meanwhile, back in Husum—and not just Husum but up and down the Columbia River Gorge, communities had become divided over whether the federal government should move forward with plans to declare the Gorge a national scenic area. Alongside that debate was another environmental issue that widened the division—placing the spotted owl on the endangered species list.

The spotted owl required large stands of old growth timber to survive, so the logging companies that had been overcutting those forests for years were now being shut out of the puny remaining stands of old growth by this annoying little bird.

When I moved into Husum, I found that the community made an honest effort to make room for everyone, even clowns and tempeh makers. Now dividing lines were being drawn, and it was a matter of us versus them. Loggers, farmers, and conservatives in general stood on one side of the line, and anyone who didn't support logging these forests to the last tree were shoved over to the other side. That included the more aggressive environmentalists, and the daring ones who chained themselves to trees, but it also included anyone suspected of sympathizing with them.

I started out as a sympathizer. As a retired wandering naturalist, how could I *not* sympathize? As things started heating up, the environmentalists started to organize small protests outside the offices of logging companies and government officials. These were poorly planned affairs, and the press rarely covered them. As the "businessman" in town, I was soon drafted to learn the fine art of pitching stories to the Portland television stations—who to call, how to emphasize the conflicts embedded in the story, that sort of thing. In those pre-internet days, people got their news through TV and newspapers, so this was an important way to influence public opinion. And since I was the one who called them, they put me on camera to explain the situation. Suddenly I was an "environmental spokesperson."

One time we pulled together a small protest in front of the Forest Service headquarters in Hood River. It was a pretty weak turn-out—maybe twelve or fifteen people walking in a slow, sad circle with their hand-painted signs. But I got a Portland TV station out to cover it, and by helping them see how to shoot the group from the right angle, they made us look like a large, angry mob. After the TV crew left, we all went home, made popcorn, and watched ourselves on the nightly news.

The most effective protest was standing in front of the logging trucks that wanted to log a grove of old growth just a short walk from my treehouse in the newly designated Columbia River Gorge National Scenic Area. Once again, the presence of the media was crucial to our success. We gathered in front of the D9 bulldozers and skidders at first light for three days in a row, and each morning I'd coaxed the TV crews out of their Portland headquarters so that their cameras were right there waiting for us. Without cameras there, the loggers would have probably pushed us aside and gotten their trees. But with cameras there, it was a standoff. When CBS picked up the blockade as a national story, the timber company finally backed off.

For three days in a row, I'd gotten Portland TV crews to drive ninety minutes through the dark to film us at the break of dawn. That was probably the highpoint of my media experience too, but the skills I honed protecting owl habitats were to prove very useful in later years.

The most controversial moment of my activist career was when I brought in a representative from Earth First to give a talk in White Salmon, just down the road from Husum. Earth First was the radical arm of the environmental movement in the late 1980s. They were known not just for blockades of logging roads, but for spiking trees, pouring sugar into gas tanks, and other acts of sabotage. Our speaker, however, was coming to talk about the importance of preserving old-growth communities. I rented out the daylight basement meeting room of a White Salmon bank, put up a few posters around town, and got a notice put in the local paper, *The Enterprise*.

On the day of the event, I noticed something peculiar when I drove past the logging company just south of Husum. They had all eight of their trucks fired up and ready to go in the parking lot. I'd never seen all their trucks in the lot at one time, much less fired up and ready to go on a Saturday night, but it made a lot more sense when I got to the bank and saw a crowd of burly men and their families forming in the parking lot. A couple of lumber companies had set up a stage at one end of the lot, and a country music band was warming up on it. They also had three blue and white picnic coolers filled with the cheapest beer money could buy.

Inside our little meeting room, the Earth First speaker had already set up a slide projector and small screen. A dozen others from the environmental side of the street were sitting quietly in their folding chairs. I greeted everyone and introduced the speaker, but before he could get started, the log trucks outside began sounding their horns. It went on for five minutes, a cloud of noise that shut us all up. When the horns stopped, a small parade of large loggers came tumbling through the door into the meeting room.

"How am I supposed to feed my family?" shouted one man—a neighbor of mine, in fact.

"This here's timber country," shouted another. "We don't need no trouble from you outside agitators. We got enough problem-types right here."

He glared at me.

"You mean to tell me," shouted another, "that saving a goddamned *owl* is more important than putting food on my family's goddamned *table*?"

It went on like that for ten minutes. Then the country music started up and the loggers drifted back outside to listen to the music, talk to each other, and drink beer.

I'd been a part of the community for almost ten years, but that was the night that put me on the map. The next week, a letter-to-the-editor appeared in *The Enterprise*:

I hear that one of those newcomer environmentalists to the White Salmon Valley lives in a treehouse so he can be closer to the owls and a tree. The treehouse must not be made of wood because he doesn't like people to cut trees to make lumber, according to what I read in the local paper.

Newcomer? Seriously? And since when did living in a tiny house of mostly scavenged lumber qualify as overconsumption and hypocrisy?

The week after that, my neighbors started hanging a series of home-made spotted owls from carefully tied nooses along my route to work. To give credit where credit is due, the level of detail in those effigies was striking. Someone was really trying to get the owls right—and that's not easy to do when barred owls are so close in appearance to spotted owls. But it was still pretty unnerving to think that my friends and I had inspired such hateful creativity. I could see that the people of Husum were going to remember my actions for a long time.

This environmental activity was a good creative outlet for me, and it fed my sense of mission for the environment. However, as the personal nature of the hostility grew, it quickly eroded my enjoyment of life in tiny, formerly friendly Husum. There wasn't the same sense of community that I'd found when I made the big leap from Forest Grove eight years earlier. The town seemed to be getting tired of me, and I was getting tired of it. The itch kept on itching.

Existential Nausea

As the 1980s wound down, Turtle Island continued its steady yet unprofitable growth. Our gross sales for 1989 were $120,000, our first time in six figures. In 1990, gross sales rose to $133,000. In spite of the continued growth, however, my restlessness with the business started to spiral me down into a deep funk. Here I was, thirty-nine years old—my life was practically over—and all I had to show for my investment in Turtle Island was a decade of frustration.

By strict financial measures, this business was a failure. I still believed in the mission of tempeh, and I didn't actually feel like a failure, either. However, it became harder to ignore the idea that I may not be cut out for this business thing. In nine years, I had taken home a *total* of $31,000 in salary. I still loved making tempeh, and the business was indeed growing as the market for plant-based proteins started to develop. But I couldn't see how Turtle Island was ever going to become profitable. It seemed like a poor bet.

Sitting one night at my desk in the old first- and second-grade classroom, I took a cold, hard look at my options. I had two:

1. Stick with the failing tempeh business. I couldn't see how Turtle Island was ever going to become profitable, so that seemed like a losing proposition. Aunt Rosie's opinion from 1980 was still looking pretty sound in 1989. Was it a good idea to sell moldy soybeans to the meat-eating American public? Probably not.

2. Throw all my efforts into finishing my coffee table book on treehouses. By then, I knew that my competitor was some kind of building contractor. I also knew that he had a contract and an advance from Houghton Mifflin. I

thought I could probably write better than a building contractor could, and I had photos of a dozen very cool treehouses, but did it really make sense to invest a lot of energy in that project when I didn't have a publisher and probably couldn't beat him to market? Probably not.

I shook my head. What would my life even look like if this tempeh business did succeed? Could I handle the workload and pressure, or would it turn my brain into mush? I didn't have any answers. All I had was questions. Tempeh had been my north star for an entire decade, and where had it gotten me? It felt like I needed a new star to follow, but I couldn't quite let go of tempeh, and I didn't quite trust the treehouse book.

So instead of making a decision, I went home to my treehouse and got just a little drunk. Drinking is good for existential nausea, right? And the next morning, now with two kinds of nausea, I went back to work. I kept my options open, which is another way of saying I avoided committing to either path. I gave most of my attention to the business, and when I could, I went to visit and photograph a new treehouse.

I knew something had to change, but apparently change would have to come to me.

Incorporation

When I brought my records to my tax guy in 1990, he asked me the same two questions that he'd been asking for many years. How much money did I lose this year? How exactly did I manage to stay in business? The answer to the first question was that I'd lost a little less than the year before. The answer to the second question was Bob, my brother and banker. He'd kept us afloat with a steady stream of short-term loans and a $20,000 investment in the business that made us partners.

This year, the tax guy said that it was probably time for Turtle Island to incorporate. We were large enough by then that any medium-sized catastrophe could bring lasting damage not just to the business but to me and my brother Bob personally. To limit liability, the tax guy recommended that we form a Subchapter S corporation.

That made sense to us, but valuing the business was hard. As my tax guy knew all too well, the business had yet to show an actual profit and wasn't likely to show one anytime soon. By those financial measures, the business wasn't worth anything. It didn't matter how proud I was of its steady growth, the top-quality tempeh we sold, or our small but growing number of devoted early adopters.

But then again, five years earlier a tofu maker in Seattle had thought we were worth $25,000, and we'd grown since then. So I picked the number $75,000 out of thin air and decided that's what the business was worth. Because of his $20,000 investment, that gave Bob twenty-seven percent ownership. That felt about right. It was twenty-seven percent of nothing, but still— twenty-seven percent. It made the burden of Bob's investment feel a little lighter.

A year earlier, I'd also gotten a check for $5,000 from my 78-year-old mother.

"You work so hard, Seth," she told me over the phone in her sweet, quavering voice. "I'm going to send you a check to help out. You can think about it as an advance against your inheritance."

I didn't really have a way to say no to that, but I'd never felt quite right about taking her money, so when we drew up the papers, I assigned Mom thirteen percent ownership of the S-corporation. I knew it was thirteen percent of nothing, but it made me feel better about the transaction and Mom thought it was sweet. Later on, this investment helped cover the medical care costs that her pension couldn't meet.

In June of 1990, the three remaining members of the Chesapeake Bay Tibbott family formed "Turtle Island Foods, Incorporated" as an S-corporation in the State of Washington. In doing so, I transferred forty percent of the company for my brother and mother's investments of $25,000. I felt guilty about taking their actual money in exchange for ownership of a business that showed no signs of turning a profit anytime soon, but they were happy with our agreement. In fact, they were proud of it.

Sue

The bigger change came to me in the form of Sue Spowart, who lived fifteen miles up the valley in Trout Lake. I met Sue at a Thanksgiving gathering there. Sue was a slim, artistic woman of many talents. She was a fantastic cook, threw pots in her small pottery shop, and kept a lush garden. Like me, she loved the outdoors and to travel. I was smitten, but I played it cool. I think I played it cool.

Sue worked for the Forest Service in Trout Lake. She had purchased a farmhouse on an acre of land in a small mountain town north of Husum for $17,000 in the early 1970s and paid it off while raising her son, Jaime. We started spending a lot of time together; sometimes up in the trees but mostly at her place. Sue was insightful, and she had no trouble telling me what she thought.

I remember telling her about how discouraged I was with tempeh. At the time, Sue had her own itch to find something to do beyond her work with the Forest Service, so she suggested that maybe she try her hand at inventing something new with tofu—pies. We'd been thinking about doing something with tofu for years, but we'd never landed on anything. I encouraged her to give it a shot.

She created three creamy tofu pies—chocolate raspberry, mocha, and my favorite, key lime. They all had a great taste and smooth texture. We sampled them out to random customers and got a strong response. People really liked them.

"This could be it," I told Sue. "This could be what Turtle Island's been waiting for."

Then I took them to a Portland lab for nutritional analysis. The results deflated us both. Sue's delicious pies were high in fat—higher in fat than regular pies with all their eggs and milk. In 1990, fat was the great evil in natural food nation, so we had to shelve the pies. Even so, the tofu pie experience opened a door in my thinking. I was still committed to tempeh as my north star, but the pies got me considering other options with tofu.

20/20 HINDSIGHT:
Don't Spread Yourself Too Thin

During the lean 1980s, I was also desperate for cash to pay salaries and expand sales. The small stream of money coming in from the tempeh business was just barely keeping us afloat. Out of necessity, I began to work on new revenue streams that would bring more money into the business. I tried expanding direct sales of tempeh to stores and restaurants in the Portland area instead of selling everything through distributors. I also tried selling tempeh products at fairs and festivals as a side business.

Selling direct to stores brought in an extra $500 per month at a time when the business was doing around $2,000 per month.

Amber Yezek and I slicing tempehroni for a Seattle pizza company in the kitchen of the Husum School, circa 1986. *(The Tofurky Company)*

Because I was already delivering products to Portland distributors like Applegate, it made some sense to add a few more weekly deliveries in exchange for that much additional revenue. The downside was that now I had to spend a whole day doing deliveries and find a place to crash overnight in Portland.

Selling tempeh at festivals and fairs took more overhead and time than selling directly did, and it didn't bring in a steady stream of revenue. We had some very good festivals that brought in hundreds of dollars, but we had some terrible ones where we lost a lot of money. The small trailer that I converted into a food truck was a headache too. Any kind of remodel is a headache, but trailers are especially so. Selling tempeh from a food truck to big crowds around the area did have a nice marketing component, but it was a huge investment that didn't really pay for itself. On top of that, it distracted us from the production business that was the core of our little enterprise.

It's a good idea to try new ideas out. Sometimes those side hustles turn into the new core of your business, as you will soon see. However, it's a bad idea to let those side hustles spread you too thin. At that point, they start to threaten the business as a whole. So be careful about that. Every now and then, step back from what you're doing and decide, maybe for the hundredth time, what business you are in so that you can devote most or all your energy to making it work.

CHAPTER SEVEN
(1991-94)

REINVENTION

I n which I climb down from the trees, get married, have a kid, and try to turn Turtle Island—or my writing career—into something that meets the needs of my new little family. Along the way, I am finally able to live up to the expectations of Mr. Business from the SBA seminar and graduate from the Be Less Stupid School of Business with a passing grade.

Bootstrappers, one of the hardest things to do when you've been following a dream through the wilderness is to edit the dream. It feels like you're selling out, and sometimes maybe you are. You be the judge of that. But if you stay true to a mission you believe in, then editing the dream based on what you've learned is really just a better way of bringing your dream into the real world.

Family

In 1991, Sue and I decided to get married. For some reason, Sue wasn't particularly interested in moving up into the trees, so after seven years of arboreal life, I turned the treehouse over to my landlord Amber and moved fifteen miles up the highway to Sue's beautiful old farmhouse in Trout Lake.

Now that the business has done as well as it has in the last two decades, people often ask Sue if I made her sign a prenup before we got married.

"Prenup!" she scoffs. "I'm the one who needed a *prenup*. I had a house. I had a job with the Forest Service. I had insurance. He was living in a *tree*."

The good news was that Sue didn't marry me for my money. The bad news was that I didn't have any money. In 1991, Turtle Island had gross sales of $152,000, and I was finally making my 1980 dream salary of $1,000 a month, so there was a glimmer of hope that Turtle Island could live up to the 1980 dream. However, the net loss that year was $30,000, which was not so hopeful.

Could I make Turtle Island both profitable and a good creative outlet? I wasn't so sure. I couldn't let go of the treehouse book.

"So go write it," Sue told me, which was great. But I also couldn't let go of the business.

"So do both," she said.

So that's what I decided to do. And a few months later, when Sue told me we had a new little turtle on the way, I committed myself to pursue both options with more creative energy than I'd given either in the previous few years. I could live on nothing comfortably enough, but that wouldn't do for my family. With a baby to think about, it was clearly time for some reinvention.

Leaving Husum

In the early 1990s, a new demographic called "windsurfers" arrived on the local scene. The eastern end of the Columbia River

Gorge has some pretty dependable wind in spring and summer, and soon the Columbia was covered with neon-bright sails and migratory windsurfers skimming from one side to the other.

On the Oregon side of the Columbia, the town of Hood River went to work creating public beaches and new businesses to support this new recreational industry. For generations, Hood River had lived and died by the harvest from the nearby orchards, especially the apples and pears. But now the town was trying to diversify with recreational dollars. On the Klickitat County side of the river, bartenders at one local bar famously put on t-shirts that said "F--- Boardheads," but without the dashes. Klickitat County had no interest in pivoting from logging and ranching to recreation. People were perfectly happy to live in the past.

As more seasonal recreation dollars began to flow into Hood River, the city decided to further diversify by offering new businesses affordable space and other incentives to bring in year-round manufacturing jobs. The Port of Hood River purchased the Graf Building, a big, concrete production plant that had once been home to a tortilla chip maker. In 1991, the Port offered to subdivide those 26,000 square feet by building out offices, mezzanines, and production space for new tenants.

It was a tempting opportunity for Turtle Island. The chip company had made some big improvements to the space, including adding floor drains, which was the number one thing I looked for in a food plant because it was so expensive to install them. With a population of 5,000 people in town, we'd have a bigger labor pool to draw from. And with I-84 running through town, we'd finally be able to get suppliers to deliver beans directly to the business—and save a *lot* of money shipping our products to market.

It felt like the perfect next move, just like Husum had felt perfect ten years earlier. But when I sketched out the budget for expanding into this larger space, it looked like we'd need to invest at least $100,000 in new equipment, which meant borrowing at least $100,000, and probably more. The rent would go up to $1,200 a month. I wouldn't be able to pull that off with another year of modest growth in our gross sales. I'd have to *double* sales in a year, two years at most. Either the universe would have to get its act together and make tempeh the next granola, or I'd have to reinvent the business into a faster moving turtle.

I talked the move over with Sue and with my brother Bob. We saw the risk, that it might not work out, that we might have nothing to show for the past eleven years, but Bob and Sue were both behind the move. They too thought that the Husum chapter had run its course and that the business needed more room to grow and reinvent itself. It was a risk, but they thought it was a risk worth taking.

In December of 1991, I signed on with the Port of Hood River and started outfitting a new tempeh plant in my corner of the building. I borrowed the $100,000 I needed from Bob and agreed to pay it back over five years, assuming I could double the business quickly. The new tempeh shop was going to be five times bigger than the 700 square feet we had in the Husum school's kitchen. I didn't need that much space, not yet, so I cut my costs a little by renting out 800 square feet to a local yoga instructor, who promptly painted her sublet with the bright colors and geometric patterns that are usually reserved for kaleidoscopes.

I outfitted the rest of the plant with new equipment that would allow me to double production and more. A small boiler ran two large kettles. I added a pasteurization cabinet, a walk-in flash freezer, a storage freezer, and a brand-new tempeh incubation room that could produce 800 pounds of tempeh every day for when we doubled sales. Upstairs was a small office, an employee break room, and storage space that would hold a whole truckload of organic soybeans.

I hauled the last load of Turtle Island gear out of Husum in May of 1992. Before I got into the truck, I took one last look around at that place that had been my home for the last eleven years. Millions of gallons of water had cascaded over Husum Falls in the last eleven years. The new us versus them dynamic had moved into the sleepy little village, but Husum itself looked unchanged. The treehouse-sized post office still stood in the center of the town next to the two-bay firehouse and its two ancient red engines. A dilapidated rental house stood across the street with the door wide open, an overgrown lawn, and no one home. A skinny dog walked slowly past the grade school's parking lot, looking neither to the left nor the right, and laid down in the shade of the church.

Don and Betty's Café had closed by then. It would sit empty for years until recreation dollars finally swam up the White Salmon to Husum. A rafting company would buy the old café and base its operations there. Shady, the shady businessman, was out of the picture. The Husum Fire Department was negotiating with the school board to buy the school and transform it into a three-bay fire station with updated engines. That seemed like a good outcome to me. Husumites would now be able to take their showers in peace.

When I looked up on the hillside to where Luther Olsen's town well stood, I saw a full-sized and completely albino deer grazing on the alfalfa around the well. I'd never seen the deer before, and I never saw it again. Was it a good omen? A little tip of the hat from a benevolent universe? I didn't have time to figure it out. I had beans to ferment. So I stepped up into the truck, pulled the door closed, remembered that this door didn't close like normal truck doors, opened it again, and this time slammed it shut—and headed down the road to the new Turtle Island.

Starting Up in Hood River

We started production in Hood River that same month, following the master plan that my business manager Dave and I had drawn up. Complete with spreadsheets and charts, our plan mapped out how the business would be able to cut costs and grow quickly over the next two years. The key to success was that Dave and I would do most of the production while at the same time running the business. We tried to unlock success with that key for about a month before throwing it away in exhaustion.

My new family: Sue, Luke, and Seth Tibbott at Moose Lake, Canada, in 1994. (Sue Tibbott)

On June 9, 1992, our son Luke was born in the tiny White Salmon hospital. It was the most amazing thing I'd ever witnessed, the most amazing experience of my life, so amazing that I almost fainted. I guess I'd thought that something as common as child-birth would be normal, but it wasn't. It was miraculous.

I took about ten days off after Luke's birth, and when I came back, there was no looking back. More than ever, I felt like I really had to rise up and become the bean winner for the family by turning Turtle Island into a real, growing business. I decided I needed to clear about $40,000 a year to meet the needs of my new little family and pay back Bob's big loan, so there was no more cottage industry for this guy. I was going to turn Turtle Island into a national brand. I was going to blow it up.

Having by then abandoned the idea that Dave and I would run the business and production ends of the operation on our own, we expanded the staff. Dave remained the business manager and bookkeeper. I handled customer service, marketing, sales, and purchasing. We had three others to oversee maintenance, logis-tics, and production. We brought in three full-time production workers from the Husum shop and added several other part-time production workers, including Jaime, Sue's son and the future CEO of The Tofurky Company, as a summer worker, and Gra-ciela, who would later become our hard-working production manager—and savior, frankly, in more than one crisis.

The Port of Hood River built out an 800-square-foot mezza-nine for offices, a lunchroom, and soybean storage. With our new production space and equipment, we made 800-pound batches of tempeh two or three times a week. On occasion, I still drove to Portland for supplies or deliveries in an old Ford Econoline, known affectionately as "the Death Van," but because we were now located just a block from an exit on I-84, most trucks didn't mind coming to us to drop off supplies or pick up product for distributors. We could now bring in 40,000 pounds of beans at a time and store them in the shop.

What stayed the same after the move from Husum to Hood River was the company vibe. With workloads so high and salary and benefits so low, I worked hard to keep things as light and fun as possible. In Husum, we regularly took breaks to go hang out at the river or race office chairs up and down the grade school's hallways. I found an online auction for a costume shop in Philadelphia that was going out of business and bought a small pallet of robes, capes, leprechaun coats, Santa suits, and superhero costumes. Anyone could use any of these when they felt moved to do so.

The fun, semi-magical vibe seemed to attract employees with at least some sense of humor, which helped to sustain the vibe, and it kept the turnover rate low. Who *doesn't* want to work at a company where the boss arrives for your interview dressed up as the Hulk? Or where you can slip into a Santa suit if you're having a bad day? Dressing up as Santa makes everything a little bit better.

In 1992, the expanded operation in Hood River raised our gross sales to $184,000. In 1993, they rose again to $209,000. That wasn't the kind of explosive growth I wanted to see from Turtle Island, but it was still growth. We were able to pay for the larger staff, make rent, and buy new equipment. By "new," I mean "new to us" and "near death" or a "piece of crap" to any reasonable person. Bob worked with us to restructure the terms of his big loan, so with his flexibility we were able to make regular payments there too. We weren't coming anywhere close to using the full production capacity of the Hood River shop, and I wasn't bringing home that $40,000, but we were getting by.

Once More to the Treehouse

Although pushing ahead with the move to Hood River took most of my time and energy in 1992, I was still committed to the treehouse book project. Building and living in the treehouse had changed my personal life, so it was easy to imagine that this book might bring the same kind of magic and change my professional life.

However, I was getting worried about my competitor. The word in the trees was that Houghton Mifflin would publish his book sometime in 1993. That meant it was time to get a contract of my own. If I could do that, I would drop everything at Turtle Island into Dave's lap and give my full attention to the book for the next year.

By then, I had done a lot of research into landing a potential publisher, but with time running out on the project I decided to skip the step of sending out a bunch of queries and instead sent a full book proposal to just one publisher, Ten Speed Press in Berkeley. I thought Ten Speed was my best bet—a big press that was willing to take risks with off-the-beaten-track titles like the *Moosewood Cookbook* series and *Vegetable Literacy*. They just *felt* right too. Their catalog had a strong flavor to it, and I thought my project was a perfect fit.

Because Dave was a computer wiz and I was not, he helped me pull together a beautiful, eighteen-page proposal complete with some of the photographs we'd taken over the years and some of the best letters of support that I'd gotten from readers of my story in *Whole Earth Review*. "Treehouse dwellers are an as-yet unchronicled segment of society," I wrote. "Writing from my own experience as a treehouse builder and dweller gives me a special insight into the arboreal projects of others." The cover letter was a masterpiece, I thought.

Then I grouped my large collection of treehouses into seven chapters:

1. Treehouses of the Rich and Famous
2. Treehouses of the Creative and Obscure
3. Treehouses and the Law
4. Portable Treehouses
5. Treehouses in the Manicured Environment
6. No Grown-Ups Allowed Treehouses
7. Treehouse Hotels

I laid out the timeline and budget I'd need to finish the manuscript and photography. It was ambitious but reasonable, I thought. Once the contract was in place with Ten Speed, I would travel to eight states to photograph treehouses and write the entire manuscript over the course of the next five months. Then I'd work with Ten Speed for the next two months after that to revise the book and lay it out for publication.

To cover my expenses for these months away from Turtle Island, I proposed a budget of $24,000. That included $2,000 a month for living expenses—a nice little bump from the $1,500 a month I was bringing home then. The rest was for office space, travel, and photography. I'd been working on this project for five years. Go big or go home, I thought.

When I finally mailed the proposal off, I felt that I'd done everything I could to make it a successful project. I was so nervous, so excited. Everyone I talked to loved the project. Everyone who'd read the proposal told me the same thing, that it was a can't-miss book. I was sure that I was about to realize my dream of becoming a writer. But Ten Speed turned me down cold with a photocopied rejection letter.

That kind of hurt. And you know what? It still kind of hurts. Having worked with a publisher on this book, I can see now that my timeline was perhaps overly ambitious, but otherwise, it was a great idea then and it's a great idea now. Ten Speed should have jumped on it. When my competitor's book finally came out—in *1994*—it was a big hit for him and Houghton Mifflin. It was the first of the four treehouse books he would put out, along with treehouse calendars that are still coming out, and his own treehouse-building show on some cable TV network. I will admit that he did a good job on all of the books and calendars, and it's not his fault that these "reality" shows are so formulaic. But that could have been me!

When Ten Speed passed on my proposal, I even reached out to my competitor to see if perhaps we might team up on a single project. If you can't beat them, join them, right? He came to Hood River and met me in the Turtle Island offices. I showed him around the plant and then sat down with him to look at the photos that Laura the photographer and I had taken over the past few years. There were a lot of treehouses in my collection that he'd never heard of.

He offered me some decent money for the collection, but I couldn't sell it to him. For one thing, my writer's dream wasn't dying easily. My parents had told me for *years* that I should be a writer, that I had a way with words, that people would like my stories. And for years, I had believed them. I still do. The treehouse book, even with Ten Speed's rejection, still seemed like the best way to make that dream come to life.

The other thing was something he told me during the tour of the shop.

"I have a friend who started this sparkling water company," he said. "Talking Rain."

"I've heard of it."

"Yeah," he said. "He's been going at it for years, just like you. He sells a lot of product, but it's not profitable, either. He loses a ton of money every year."

That hurt too, and since it didn't seem appropriate to put on a Santa suit in that moment, it kept on hurting as we looked over my photos and he offered me money.

"No," I told him. "Not for sale."

In hindsight, I probably should have kept shopping my project to other publishers, even if it meant publishing my book after my competitor did. Being first in the market with a ground-breaking product gives you a big advantage, but I've learned since then that there's something to be said about a healthy category raising all the boats. Just because one book came out and succeeded first doesn't mean that another book with other treehouses, stories, and approaches wouldn't have sold well too.

Whatever. The fact is that while the treehouse book lived on for years as dream, I stopped pursuing it as a project after Ten Speed's undignified rejection. I picked up my bleeding ego from the floor, and from that point on, I gave all my creative energy to Turtle Island.

KISS, But Not the Band

When I turned my full focus to the tempeh shop in Hood River, it was easy to see both the challenge and the way forward for Turtle Island. The challenge was building income so I could pay back Bob's $100,000 loan, cover the expanded overhead, and bring home more income for my family. Sue was by then looking for a way to get out of her job at the Forest Service, so building up the business would help her do that too. The way forward was all the extra capacity we had in this new shop. We could scale up quickly to a thousand pounds of tempeh a day if we had someone to sell it to.

My first idea for how to build demand was to develop secondary tempeh products. We had already started down this road with the introduction of Superburgers, which were marinated soy/rice tempeh patties you could grill. They were good sellers, but it was a seasonal product. How else might we repackage tempeh to make life easier and tastier for our overworked customers?

Because the most common way for people to cook tempeh was stir-frying, we invented a product in the fall of 1992 called "KISS." KISS was an acronym for "Keep It Simple Stirfry." Because no one knew how to cook tempeh properly, they often cut it into large, one-inch cubes without marinating it—like tofu. That was okay, but it didn't do tempeh justice. With KISS, we cut the tempeh into half-inch cubes and marinated it in three different marinades— Lemon Teriyaki, Garlic Italian, and Spicy Szechuan. All the customer had to do was take the KISS tempeh out of its plastic tub, dump it into a wok or skillet, and sauté. Voila! The perfect, delicious stir fry, and a big improvement over tempeh on its own.

I thought it was a brilliant product, a sure hit, something that met a market need in a new and interesting way—just like I'd learned over the past twelve years while working on my MBA from the Be Less Stupid School of Business. KISS felt like my master's thesis, something I could show Mr. Businessman from the Small Business Administration seminar all those years earlier. This was something that could raise the profile of tempeh and change the market.

"See?" I could tell the SBA guy. "I'm not an idiot after all!"

We went all in on marketing. We built a cool "KISSing booth" for the giant Expo West trade show, the same show where I'd first met Al Jacobson, "The Wizard of Foods." We printed slick packaging for the product and made colorful sell sheets and t-shirts to hand out. I went full-on businessman too, wearing the finest suit and tie that JCPenney had to offer.

And it worked too, at first. We got good orders from the Expo West show. We got some easy press. People loved the catchy name and the concept. My little MBA master's thesis seemed to be a hit. However, after the market gave my KISS thesis a closer look, it handed it back to me with a C–. The strong early orders never translated into strong follow-up orders. The orders dropped in the coming months and then stopped entirely.

One of the main problems with the KISS tempeh was during the three weeks it took KISS to move through the distribution channels to stores and then customers, the tempeh soaked up lots

"Keep It Simple Stirfry." Marinated tempeh in Lemon Teriyaki, Spicy Szechuan, and Garlic Italian. (Laura Ewig)

of marinade. The longer it sat on the shelf, the more marinade the KISS cubes absorbed. About thirty days into its sixty-day shelf life, the KISS tempeh lost its firm tempeh texture and became way too salty. A lot of people tried it, which was great, but most of them only tried it once. The concept was right, but the product didn't live up to its promise.

I was disappointed, of course, but something changed with KISS. Even though KISS never made it, it felt like I'd still completed my degree from Be Less Stupid. I could tell I had arrived somehow. I had taken a shot at something entirely new, a cutting-edge idea, and I'd had fun with it too. That was important.

On top of that, I'd learned something else from the experience—authenticity. I didn't have enough of it yet. I was still holding back, still trying to look the part of "businessman" as defined by the SBA guy and all the worker bees in the other Expo West booths. What was I doing wearing a suit and tie? I never wore a suit or tie—except for the occasional Santa suit or the little black tie that went with the leprechaun costume. I couldn't think of anything phonier than me in a regular suit and a tie. Whether people at the show liked KISS or not, they could tell that I was just acting a part, and not very well. That was going to have to change.

It wasn't just me, of course. Looking at the other natural food companies of the day, I saw the same kind of phoniness. It wasn't just the abundance of ties and conservative attire, either. The whole universe of natural foods marketing was so humorless and dull. As I'd gotten to know more people in the business, I'd learned that however drab their marketing and clothing was, most of them were just as fun and weird as me. That dissonance jumped out at me that year.

Only the Wizard of Foods, himself, Al Jacobson, was bucking that trend and having fun being the wacky, authentic person behind the Garden of Eatin' brand. As KISS slowly faded into the sunset, I resolved to start being the businessman I truly was—creative and whimsical—and to stop trying to fit myself or my products to match what I thought the world expected from me.

Contracting More Business

A second way to use more production capacity is to contract some of that capacity out to other food producers. That's what I tried next. I'd met a nice guy at a trade show who worked in the research and development lab at Con Agra. He and his wife were vegans in their thirties, and they knew all about tempeh. His job was to develop vegan products for the Healthy Choice line at Con Agra. He was looking for IQF—individually quick-frozen—cubes of tempeh that they could run through their machines and pump into Healthy Choice meals at high speeds.

This sounded like a perfect opportunity to change the fortunes of the business. We had just developed our ill-fated KISS product, so we knew how to cube tempeh. We didn't have a spiral freezer unit to create IQF tempeh cubes, though. That cost $600,000 that we didn't have, but that was a problem I was sure we could overcome. We also didn't have a conveyorized deep fryer that would have made the tempeh so much tastier to eat—another $600,000 we didn't have—but I told myself that wouldn't be a problem because of our tasty marinade.

We began with test batches for Con Agra focus groups. First we cut and marinated the tempeh cubes. Then we put them on baking pans to freeze overnight. This worked great except that the marinade made the cubes freeze together into one pan-sized cube that then had to be broken apart into cube-sized cubes. As you can imagine, that was a hassle. It took forever to put together a shipment of cubes for testing, and when the focus groups tested them out, nobody really liked the taste because it hadn't been fried first. Lacking the right equipment, we weren't ready to contract for the volume of tempeh that Con Agra wanted.

I was starting to get nervous about how this move to Hood River was going to work out when I got a call from a tofu and tempeh maker in Santa Cruz. He had wised up to the tempeh gig and decided it was way too much work to keep making tempeh in their tofu kitchens. He had a good customer base, though, and wanted to keep their customers happy. So would Turtle Island be interested making their tempeh for them?

Yes, Turtle Island *would* be interested in making their tempeh for them. We had the two main requirements for co-packing—lots of unused production capacity and lots of debt. So we quickly signed on to make their three lines of tempeh. I made them great tempeh at a good price and filled up a nice chunk of my unused production capacity. I didn't have to worry about sales or marketing or distribution. All I had to do was cash their checks. It was a good deal for everyone.

For a food production business, co-packing can be one of the more dangerous things you can do. The food production world is full of horror stories of co-packers suddenly dropping someone's line to pursue a more lucrative line elsewhere—or even worse, learning how to make your product, dropping it, and then coming out with their own version of it. I've seen more than one company fail because of a bad co-packing agreement.

However, *providing* co-packing has some nice advantages. The number one advantage for us was filling up our empty capacity with production time and getting paid without having to do any sales or marketing. That's how we won on this win-win agreement. The tempeh makers from Santa Cruz won as well because they could concentrate on producing more lucrative lines in their shop.

A First Glimpse of the Wild Tofurky

In 1994, our gross sales grew to $253,000. Turtle Island still wasn't profitable, just like Talking Rain apparently, but it felt like we were finally heading in that direction instead of running in place. We were making loan payments to Bob and adding more staff to help with production and marketing. I took home over $21,000 in 1994, which was not the $40,000 I wanted but still— so much money!

Sue continued to work for the Forest Service while working on secret new recipes for Turtle Island. One of her inventions was a new tempeh burger. It tasted good, but we both thought there was something off about it. I couldn't put my finger on it. A week later, Sue had it figured out.

"Thanksgiving," she said. "It tastes like Thanksgiving, not summer."

That was exactly right. So we had to put that one to the side, along with her tasty tofu pies.

Thanksgiving had always been a weird holiday for me food-wise. Growing up, I never really cared for it. I didn't like much of anything that my aunt put on her Thanksgiving table. I'd pick at some mashed potatoes and a few rolls with butter was about all I would eat, much to my aunt's dismay. I would have nothing to do with the green beans, salad, turkey, or even the pumpkin pie.

"The best compliment you can give a cook," my aunt told me, "is to eat everything on your plate."

My response was to carefully fold my napkin over my plate in order to hide the food I didn't want to eat, which was most of it. How I dreaded that meal! And as it turns out, I wasn't alone. I began to notice another clue from the universe about the future, and this time it came to me through the funny pages.

After Luke was born in 1992, I developed a little Sunday morning ritual with him. I'd put him on my back and then he and I would walk the quarter mile from our little house in Trout Lake to the Trout Lake General Store to buy the *Sunday Oregonian* newspaper. This was back when there were still newspapers. Then we'd walk back to the house and I'd take my time paging through the paper.

I read the news. I read the sports. I carefully scanned the classified ads for used restaurant equipment. I saved the Sunday comics for last. As Thanksgiving rolled around in 1994, I noticed something in the funny pages. The comics were filled with jokes about tofu and turkeys. I remember one that asked, "Do you want dark tofu or white tofu?" Hilarious. There were maybe a half-dozen of them all poking fun at vegetarians with references to tofu. What was going on?

It resonated with me too, which was even weirder. The cartoons were poking fun at vegetarians in the same way that my friends had poked fun at me for *decades* of Thanksgivings over my generally unsuccessful turkey alternatives. There was the year of the stuffed pumpkin back in the 1970s, for example. I filled a large pumpkin with brown rice, Brussels sprouts, broccoli, and other veggies. It was festive and cooked well, but it was more of a side dish than a turkey alternative, with no protein, not even tempeh, which was still waiting for me to discover it.

Then there was the gluten roast I made as a turkey alternative. This was before you could buy vital wheat gluten with the starch already separated from the protein part of the wheat. To create my gluten roast, I had to knead the gluten in water for *hours*, trying with limited success to remove the starch to reveal the lovely, soft and stretchy wheat protein. It didn't go well. The finished roast was entirely inedible. It turned into a kind of wheat-based cobblestone that couldn't be cut with an electric knife, much less chewed by human teeth.

Reading the comics that Sunday with Luke on my lap, I thought about all those frustrating Thanksgivings.

"What do you think, Luke?" I said. "Are there enough people like us out there now? Is this a niche that needs to be filled with an edible alternative?"

Luke looked up and asked me for a graham cracker. I took that as a yes.

That same week, I had another experience that told me I was definitely onto something. While delivering some tempeh to my friends Hans and Rhonda at Portland's Higher Taste vegetarian deli, I noticed that Hans was making something I'd never seen before. He mashed up a bowl of tofu with herbs and spices. Then he put the mixture into a cheesecloth-lined colander and punched a cavity into it with his fist. He filled the cavity with stuffing, flipped it onto a baking sheet, and put it in the oven.

"What is that?" I asked him.

He smiled.

"Stuffed tofu roasts," he said. "For the holidays. Twenty-five dollars!"

He explained that he'd been doing this on a special-order basis for some of his customers who were looking for a delicious and meatless alternative for Thanksgiving. He hoped to sell at least fifty in Portland that year. Everything Hans made tasted amazing, so I paid for mine on the spot. Was this the turkey alternative I'd been dreaming of for the last twenty years?

Hans's roast didn't even make it to our Thanksgiving table. Sue and I couldn't wait. We baked it as soon as I got home and dug in. As usual, Hans didn't disappoint. The tofu was nicely seasoned. The texture was firm enough that we could cut the roast into pie-shaped wedges, and the wedges didn't fall apart. The stuffing was perfect. There was even a nice orange/cranberry sauce to go with it. Sue and I looked at each other across the table.

This was big. This was the future. We could tell.

And this time, I could tell that I was going to be ready for the future. I may have gotten a C– on my KISS master's thesis, but that's still a passing grade. I was now smart enough to see that for Turtle Island to make it, I'd have to do something with tofu. More importantly, this time I'd take the initiative and bring my invention to the world instead of waiting for the world to come to me.

There was still a part of me that resisted the idea of pivoting toward tofu because of the tempeh dream I'd been pursuing all these years. It had been a point of pride to stay true to tempeh. And I knew that my crew at Turtle Island had no interest in moving away from tempeh. That's what they knew. But this was bigger than that. I could tell that this was opening the door to the real reinvention of Turtle Island as a business and me as a businessman. I didn't see any of the specifics, but I knew the future would have something to do with tofu and turkey.

20/20 HINDSIGHT:
Be Patient but Not Stupid

People like to tell each other to "do what you love, and the money will follow." Maybe, but how much money will that be? And how quickly will it follow? In my case, the money that followed my tempeh dream was a low three-figures monthly salary that trickled in for the better part of a decade. Sitting there on the pier of dreams waiting for a bigger ship to come in, I had a lot of time to think about what I was doing and whether it was worth the wait.

The treehouse book started as something fun to do, a way to be creative while waiting for my Turtle Island tempeh ship to come in. However, because of my impatience with tempeh, it soon morphed into a Plan B that started to take time and creativity away from my slow-moving Plan A. It was a sexy young temptation with no downsides that I was willing to consider. That's why I was so crushed when it dumped me for my competitor.

From where I stand now, however, I'm glad that I ended up back on the Turtle Island pier with no Plan B. I may have thought then that I could pursue the dream of becoming a treehouse book writer *and* the dream of becoming a successful tempeh magnate, the reality was there was only enough of me to pursue one dream at a time.

When I returned to Plan A, though, I came back to do more than wait for my ship to come in. I looked for ways to speed up its arrival. One of those ways was pivoting just a little bit away from tempeh to see what I could do with tofu as a plant-based protein. And although it would still be a few years in its coming, that pivot is what opened the door for my Tofurky moment. That's when the money finally followed the dream.

When we start our businesses, our visions are usually founded more on hunches than on experience or any other kind of real-world data. They begin when we're at the most stupid point of our business selves. So while it's good to be patient with your dream, to stick with it because it has to work, it's also good to keep refining that dream as you become less stupid about business. If your brain shows you a more profitable way to follow your dream, follow it. Don't stay as stupid as you were when you started. Getting stuck in rigid thinking, even your own inspired rigid thinking, might keep your ship from ever coming in.

You'll read all about that in the next chapter.

THE TOFURKY MOMENT

I n which everything changes quickly—or at least quickly from the perspective of someone who just spent fifteen years figuring out how to run a business. This time, when a benevolent universe gives me a clue about the future, I don't wait around for the future to come to me. Without giving up on tempeh as a great source of plant-based protein, Turtle Island pivots toward an underserved demographic of vegans and vegetarians who are tired of browsing the side dishes at holiday meals while everyone else eats turkey.

Bootstrappers, when you see your moment arrive, jump on it with both feet. Jump on it even if you know that mistakes will be made. You can correct those mistakes—in fact, it's easier for you to make corrections because you're closer to the ground and more nimble than corporations or big venture capital shops are—but you can't make the big moment wait for you while you organize your desk or do whatever it is you do to make yourself feel like you're in control of things. Be smart, bootstrapper, but jump on it.

The First Tofurky

In early 1995, I went back to Hans at Higher Taste and talked with him about teaming up to produce a plant-based alternative to roasted turkey, something that could be frozen and shipped to stores. At this point, Turtle Island was selling tempeh up and down the West Coast, from San Diego to Vancouver, BC, but not much further east than Spokane, Washington. I thought this could be the product that would push our distribution into the east.

Hans liked the idea, so we agreed to work together to have something ready for Thanksgiving 1995. The Higher Taste would make the tofu roasts and gravy. Turtle Island would provide tempeh "drummettes," buy all the materials and packaging, and sell the product through our current distributors and hopefully some new distributors further east.

You remember those Thanksgiving-flavored tempeh burgers that Sue created in the last chapter? Of course, you do. That's what we used for the drummettes—the plant-based dark meat of the turkey alternative. The main ingredients were textured soy protein, grated soy tempeh, carrots, wild rice, and cranberries. We then stamped this mix into shape on a burger patty machine, but instead of making it into a burger shape, we ordered a custom drumstick-shaped plate and found a co-packer to stamp and bake them for us.

By summer, things were coming together for the holiday feast. We had two sizes of the roast from Higher Taste, and because we weren't limited by the anatomy of an actual turkey, we then added four or eight tempeh drummettes to the two sizes of roast. Hans added a golden gravy made from nutritional yeast, improving upon a recipe first pioneered at the Farm. We took it all to a studio in Portland for some beautiful product photos. We were all set to start laying out brochures in advance of holiday sales. There was only one thing missing—a name for this creation.

First Tofurky Feast; plated 1995. *(Tutle Island Foods, Inc.)*

Hans, Rhonda, and I had been going around and around for months about what to call this new product. Hans and Rhonda pushed for something descriptive like "Meatless Stuffed Tofu Roast" because this was something new. They reasoned that people needed to know what the product offered just from reading the name. That approach made sense, of course, but it didn't roll off the tongue. It didn't engage the imagination like I wanted. It wasn't fun.

I kept thinking back to Al Jacobson and his blue corn chips. There was a businessman who had fun with his business and trusted his finely tuned business intuition. As much as a descriptive name made logical sense to me, my own business intuition told me to go for something more colorful, something that could create some buzz of its own. I pushed for the name "Tofurky."

I'd first seen the word "tofurkey," with an "e," at a deli counter in one of the Portland stores I delivered tempeh to back in 1981. I hadn't seen that sandwich or name in years, but just to be safe, I called the sandwich shop to check if it had been trademarked. No, they told me. They'd stopped using the name years ago and didn't have any particular attachment to it. I was free to use it if I wanted to. However, to avoid any possible confusion between our new product and their now-defunct tofu sandwiches, I suggested that we drop the "e."

I also wanted to drop the "e" because "Tofurkey" had eight letters and "Tofurky" had seven. That meant we could create an 800 number for it—1 (800) TOFURKY. The internet was still a baby used mostly by nerds in 1995. The main ways people interacted with companies was through toll-free telephone numbers or writing actual letters and mailing them through the postal system.

As the deadlines for getting our marketing together neared, we remained stuck over what to call it. Almost everyone sided with Hans and Rhonda, by the way, including my colleagues at Turtle Island. They were more blunt about it too.

"It's a stupid name," said one of the managers, who shall remain nameless for his or her own protection. "It sounds like a sneeze. 'Tofurky! Gesundheit!' If you want to be taken seriously, Seth, use a serious name."

My intuition told me otherwise. I thought it was catchy, funny. Nobody was doing funny in natural foods back then, but funny sure worked everywhere else. That was how I wanted Turtle Island to present itself as we moved forward, and this seemed like the perfect opportunity to try out this new approach. What did we have to lose? It wasn't like my *non*humorous marketing was getting us anywhere. I quietly hired a trademark lawyer to see if the name was available to trademark. He called me back the next day.

"Great mark!" he said. "Want me to register it?"

I knew that Hans and almost everyone else wasn't going to like it, but Turtle Island was ultimately responsible for selling this product outside of the Portland market. We also had more dollars at risk in the venture.

"Yes," I told him. We were taking this holiday roast to market as Tofurky.

Next came the matter of pricing our new product. The smaller Tofurky came with a pound and a half of stuffed tofu roast, four of Sue's tempeh drummettes, and eight ounces of mushroom gravy for $24.95. The larger Tofurky offered a three-pound roast, eight drummettes, and sixteen ounces of gravy for $34.95. Back then, the general rule for pricing products in the freezer case was to keep the price under $3.99. Tofurky, however, was not just a meal. It was a holiday feast. The pricing made everyone nervous, but my business intuition told me that this wasn't the time to underprice a new product just to generate sales. Our costs to produce the larger feast were more than $13 a piece. We had to price it that high just to cover costs.

With the name and pricing in place, it was time to market this amazing new product. Our packaging left a lot to be desired. It was a plain white cardboard box with a black and white computer printed label that said "Tofurky—The Delicious Vegetarian Holiday Alternative." Although the package was boring, the rest of the marketing program was pretty slick for 1995. Stores that agreed to take on this Thanksgiving newcomer with the funny name and high price were offered the following:

- 100 colorful brochures describing the product
- An in-store demo
- A full color, framed photo of the finished product
- A press release to send out to local media
- Line art and copy for ads in newsletters and posters

"We believe that this product has great potential of filling an unmet niche in the natural food world," the cover letter said. "It's a delicious, satisfying, and festive feast for the vegan and vegetarians among us who are currently left only with the choice of eating side dishes or pretending that turkey is a vegetable."

As compelling as our marketing pitch was, most of the retailers—even in our hometown of Portland—weren't interested. The largest chain of natural food stores in Portland took a pass even though they'd been selling Turtle Island tempeh and Higher Taste sandwiches for more than a decade. Smaller stores were still a hard sell but proved to be slightly more open to the idea of a turkey alternative. In the end, 500 frozen Tofurkys made it onto the shelves in Portland and Seattle for Thanksgiving that year.

The two stores who saw the greatest potential in Tofurky were both co-ops, Food Front in Portland and Puget Consumers Co-op in Seattle. Food Front in particular did a great job advertising the product. On Saturday, November 11, they held the first Tofurky tasting demo anywhere and took special orders from customers. People were used to making special orders for turkeys at that time, so the store put up the glossy Tofurky photos and brochures right next to the turkey ordering desk. They also sent out our press release to local Portland media outlets. Two different TV stations were interested enough to send camera crews sent to film people eating Tofurkys on Thanksgiving Day.

On Thanksgiving Day, Sue and I were getting ready to head over to our usual Thanksgiving gathering of retired naturalists just down the road when the phone rang. It was Hans, and he was excited. Oregon Public Broadcasting had picked up the Tofurky story from Food Front. A reporter had been on the air in the home of local vegetarians, asking them about their Tofurky.

"It's great!" they all said.

An hour later, which is how long it takes to prepare to go anywhere with a three-year-old, we were heading out the door when Hans called again. He was even more excited. The Channel 8 news team had come out to his and Rhonda's house and filmed them cutting up the Tofurky roast. The story was set to air that night.

Having spent all of my business life in the obscure corner of the market reserved for tempeh, this was nuts. I'd gotten a few tiny articles in the *Oregonian* and *Hood River News*. The White Salmon *Enterprise* had featured our Husum operation for its local readership. This was different. This was my first taste of actual buzz. It felt like an earthquake, but a good one, a benevolent one. I guess earthquake might not be the right metaphor, but the ground was clearly shifting below my feet.

That same week, the *New Yorker* magazine ran a full-page cartoon under the heading "Happy Surrogate Thanksgiving from the makers of Rock Hard Tofu." It included a sculpted tofu cake in the shape of a turkey that was to be baked for four hours at 375 degrees Fahrenheit. The artist clearly didn't think anyone would be foolish enough to actually try to market something like that, but here I was! The *New Yorker* cartoon was indicative of how most people looked at plant-based foods in 1995—with derision. This was especially true when plant-based foods challenged traditional paradigms like eating turkey on Thanksgiving. Tofurky quickly became a poster child for plant-based foods, making inroads into American culture before there were other plant-based products to deride.

In December, the similar-to-an-earthquake buzz continued. All stores that got in on the Thanksgiving sales were thrilled to keep selling the product, and several new ones brought Tofurky in for Christmas. Puget Consumers Co-op had done so well with Thanksgiving sales that they set up the first Tofurky hotline to take Christmas orders. We ended up selling 818 Tofurkys in 1995, grossing a little over $13,000. As usual, we had done what we did best and lost money on the product, but this time the buzz made it feel different, like it wasn't business as usual even if we'd lost money as usual.

We hadn't set up our toll-free number for 1995, so instead we asked for feedback by enclosing a self-addressed, stamped postcard with every Tofurky we sent out. As these cards started coming in, time stopped for me. The feedback was almost entirely positive, and some of it was ecstatic.

"I've been waiting twenty years for this product," wrote one customer. "I don't have to feel like a second-class citizen at the Thanksgiving table anymore!"

People *loved* the concept of having a high-protein centerpiece for their Thanksgiving tables. In fact, they loved the concept even more than they loved the product. For fifteen years, I'd been following a great product that lacked an attractive concept—mold being mold and all. That hadn't taken me anywhere. In fact, I wasn't sure I was even on a road that would even get me to the suburbs outside of Profitability. Tofurky was different. It was a great concept first, a concept that a growing number of vegetarians had been waiting for. That, I thought, is how you get to profitability.

As far as the product went, the feedback was less ecstatic. One complaint was the high price. We expected that even though, ounce for ounce, Tofurky was priced the same as a ten-ounce pack of Boca burgers selling at $3.99. An unexpected complaint was about the size—especially the size of the larger Tofurky. It turned out that you rarely had eight vegetarians or vegans at a Thanksgiving gathering—or even four. Most of the time, you had one or two people who needed something to eat other than the turkey that everyone else was eating. Several responses also raised concerns about the texture of the tofu roast. Because most of these Tofurkys were sold frozen, the texture of the tofu had changed in the thawing and cooking process. The roast became spongy, which is not a texture that people look for in meat substitutes.

This was all great feedback, and it gave me a lot of direction in planning how to redesign the product to make it as great as the concept in 1996.

The Second Tofurky Recipe

New products are like children. They take a lot of work to raise, and in spite of your best efforts, you never know how they will turn out. Not all kids grow up to be astronauts. Although Tofurky was only a couple months old, it was already looking like astronaut material. I hadn't seen anything like it from the other product children I'd launched over the prior fifteen years. As good as I was at producing products that lost money, I had a hunch that maybe, just maybe, this would be the kid who could take care of me in my old age.

We had stumbled onto what every marketer dreams of—an undiscovered niche of passionate customers who were not being served. The timing was right too. The federal government had just allowed soy products with 25mg of soy protein per serving to make a health claim on their labels. However, if Tofurky's potential was going to be fulfilled, I knew the recipe had to improve.

The biggest thing that needed to change was the texture, which I soon learned is the hardest thing to get right with all meat alternatives. The texture was fine in the fifty Tofurkys that Hans refrigerated and sold around Portland, but all of the Tofurky Feasts we sold had to be frozen before they were shipped. Because of the high water content, tofu doesn't freeze well. Its soft, creamy texture becomes spongy and full of holes when it thaws. The second problem was that the tofu-roast recipe wasn't scalable. Hans and a team of four workers could only produce 100 to 150 holiday roast Tofurkys per eight-hour shift. Every roast cost four dollars in labor alone.

Hans and I met right after the holidays and agreed that the recipe had to change for the 1996 version of Tofurky. One idea was to go with a turkey-flavored baked tofu. I called a tofu maker in Seattle whose baked tofu I admired, the same one who'd offered to buy me out for $25,000 ten years earlier, and he agreed to take a look at it. Hans developed a marinade from a natural vegetarian flavor. We vacuum-sealed two-pound blocks of thinly sliced tofu with this marinade, then baked and packaged it. Once again, Hans produced a great-tasting roast. Because the baked tofu was drier than the previous unbaked roast, it froze better too. It wasn't perfect, but it was definitely better.

I found a co-packer for the stuffing and gravy and a different co-packer for the tempeh drummettes. Then we packaged it all up

Tofurky™

A Delicious Vegetarian Holiday Feast

Whether you are seeking to offer a meatless option for a portion of your holiday table or are planning a complete vegan feast, we think Tofurky will satisfy and amaze all who try it.

WHAT IS TOFURKY™? Tofurky™ is a pre-baked vegetarian feast designed to be the delicious centerpiece of your holiday meal. It consists of four parts: 2 pounds Organic, Specially Seasoned, Baked Tofu; 8 Hearty Tempeh Drumettes; 15 oz. Heavenly Golden Mushroom Gravy; and 1½ pounds Moist Cranberry-Walnut Stuffing. Each Tofurky™ is 100% vegan, cooks in less than 30 minutes and tastes FABULOUS!

HOW DO WE MAKE IT? We season Premium Island Spring Extra Firm Tofu with a special flavor blend made with all natural, vegetarian ingredients. Then we marinate and bake the tofu to golden perfection. The taste is unique and speaks to taste buds you never knew existed! There is nothing remotely similar to this anywhere on the market.

HOW ABOUT THE TEMPEH DRUMETTES? Included in your Tofurky™ are the unique Drumettes, a dark filet made of grated organic tempeh, tvp (textured vegetable protein), organic wild rice, cranberries and carrots, seasoned and carved into yummy shaped drumsticks.

IS THERE MORE? To tie together the two distinct flavors of the Baked Tofu and Tempeh Drumettes, we have added

1996 version of Tofurky. *(Turtle Island Foods, Inc.)*

in a much prettier cardboard box that nobody was going to miss on the shelf. Our new and improved Tofurky came in one size only with two pounds of marinated, organic baked tofu, eight tempeh drummettes, sixteen ounces of golden mushroom gravy, and sixteen ounces of moist, cranberry-walnut stuffing.

The 1996 Tofurky was still bigger than most people wanted, and we still had to price it around thirty dollars just to cover costs. To counter the cost, our marketing bragged that Tofurky was able to "feed, satisfy, and amaze eight to ten hungry adults," ignoring the feedback we'd received that most Thanksgiving feasts were serving Tofurky to a smaller number of vegans and vegetarians. We had listened well to those customers who wanted a better texture, but we had not yet fully heard the demand for a smaller, less expensive product. I hadn't figured out yet that for the most part, people shop price points, not value per pound.

Ramping Up

That fall was pretty challenging. Part of the challenge was that Sue and I were both working long hours to make ends meet while raising Luke, our precocious four-year-old. Our goal was to spend as much time with Luke as possible, so we did a lot of scheduling magic to make that happen.

I took off Mondays to hang with Luke, which soon became the best day of the week for me. Our pattern was to get up early and drive thirty minutes to the Hood River Library. Luke and I would pick out the week's reading material. Then we'd go to the local park so that Luke could run around the park screaming with the other small children. Then we'd finish the morning off with a trip to Andrew's Pizza for lunch. Sue took off Fridays to spend with Luke. They had their own playtime rituals. For Tuesday, Wednesday, and Thursday, I went into work around ten after dropping Luke off at a local babysitter. Sue went to work early on those days and picked Luke up around 3:00 p.m.

When *not* hanging with Luke, Sue and I both had to be super productive at work. I had a hard time getting home before 7 or 8 p.m. on most nights. October through December had formerly been our slowest months, but now they were the most intense. At Turtle Island, our well-behaved tempeh product children continued their steady, polite, manageable growth. Tofurky, though, was the product child who banged pots together and screamed for more attention as we tried to handle all the promotion, packaging, and selling.

One of our goals for 1996 was to broaden the distribution of Tofurky. Even though we'd only sold 818 Tofurkys in 1995, the Tofurky buzz, fueled partly by the media attention, was spreading to other parts of the country. Customers started to ask their retailers if they had Tofurky, retailers started to ask distributors if they had Tofurky, and distributors started to call me for a change. Our first East-Coast distributor was Cornucopia Natural Foods in Connecticut. We shipped their roasts frozen on refrigerator trucks, and they sold out before Thanksgiving.

Knowing that there were still thousands of prospective customers who'd be stuck eating side dishes at Thanksgiving, I walked outside and across the yard to the house of my neighbor, former business manager, and computer wizard, Dave. By then, Dave had seen the potential of the internet and left his job at Turtle Island to create his own online company, the Simple Living Network, which he ran out of his living room. In just a few short years, Dave had built a successful business that helped people escape the rat race by simplifying their lives.

"Do you want to try to sell Tofurkys on the internet?" I asked.

"Sure," he said. "I can do that. Simple."

I was thrilled when Dave agreed to help us sell Tofurkys. Because it required overnight FedEx shipping, these Tofurkys were going to be expensive, costing $49.95 delivered anywhere in the continental United States. We set up the 1-888-TOFURKY number, and Dave created an online order page. After an exhaustive search, Dave also found a company that would work with us to process credit card orders, which wasn't really a thing yet in those days. Once that was in place, Dave was ready to sell Tofurkys to the thirty percent of US homes that had a computer in them.

The Washington Post caught wind of our online Tofurkys and published an article in their Health section—"Meatless Thanksgiving? Try a Tofurky." The reporter who interviewed me had a hard time moving away from the $49.95 price point. I tried to explain about how the American food system was built on the economies of scale, with heavy government subsidies given to animal agriculture but none for the poor Tofurky farmers. When humor didn't work, I got more technical. These Tofurkys were being shipped directly to people's homes, overnight, over the holidays. FedEx didn't provide that service on the cheap.

"But $49.95?" he asked. "Really?"

"Look," I said. "It would cost the same to ship an actual turkey overnight."

"Okay," he said. "I get that. But $49.95 is still a lot of money."

When the article came out, his continuing emphasis on the high price didn't suppress sales. They shot right up. I saw for myself that most publicity is good publicity.

With help from the press and word of mouth, the wild Tofurky traveled fast that fall. For a small company like ours, getting the media to talk about our product for free was pure marketing gold. To mine more gold, I drew up two press releases that fall. We mailed and faxed one generic release to every outlet we could think of. We also wrote a release that stores could use by filling in a few blanks with their contact info and sending it to local press. Both worked magically.

However, the biggest media hits of 1996 were national stories that came without us doing anything to get them. The first was the *Washington Post* story. The second story came from a guy named Phil Lempert, TV's "Supermarket Guru," who had spotted a Tofurky box in a Southern California store. On a *Today Show* segment, the Supermarket Guru included Tofurky as one of the five innovative Thanksgiving products to hit the market that year. Without us doing a thing, he introduced tens of millions of people to the highly innovative Tofurky.

Later, the CBS *This Morning* show traveled to the Farm Sanctuary to do a Thanksgiving story. Lorri Bauston, co-founder of the Farm Sanctuary, had cooked up a Tofurky dinner and plated it perfectly, explaining to Harry Smith and his millions of viewers that Tofurky was a meat-free—and delicious—Thanksgiving alternative.

All three of these national stories amazed us. The value of this free advertising amounted to hundreds of thousands of dollars. For our small company of a dozen people, it was a little hard to process. It felt like a door was opening to a future, and in that future, it looked like Tofurky might become a part of the Thanksgiving landscape.

The height of our holiday stress came on the Monday before Thanksgiving. None of the buyers at stores and none of the distributors knew how much of this new product to order. Some stores tried to work around the problem by asking customers to special-order Tofurkys, but the problem was that by the time those stores ordered their special orders through the distributor, the distributor was already sold out and had nothing to ship. Most distributors then had the bad manners to tell these out-of-luck stores that the shortage was due to their supplier—us—being out of stock. The retailers then called us at 1-888-TOFURKY to complain, usually to me. With Thanksgiving only a few days away, I overnighted Tofurkys to several retailers and even a few customers. I had to do that at a loss, but I told myself it was a trust-building exercise.

Meanwhile, back at the Simple Living Network, Dave had sold 300 Tofurkys online. Those also had to be shipped out that same pre-Thanksgiving Monday. We put a FedEx label on each Tofurky package and loaded all 300 packages onto a pallet for the FedEx truck to pick up at 4:00 p.m. and take to Portland for the evening plane to the Memphis hub. But November is a dodgy weather month in the northern latitudes, and when weather held up the FedEx pick-up, there was only one number to call: 1-888-TOFURKY.

The only quiet part of that fall was that the toll-free number wasn't exactly ringing off the hook. We did get calls from frustrated retailers and shoppers, and we took some online orders, but for the most part there wasn't a whole lot of phone traffic. After getting those free stories in the national media, the phone silence didn't make any sense.

But then I had a thought. What if you dialed 1-888-TOFURKE instead of 1-888-TOFURKY? I tried it, and a woman answered.

"This is Leah at Leah's Hair and Nails," she said, "How can I help you?"

"Hello," I said. "This is Seth from Turtle Island Foods in Oregon. We make a product called Tofurky, and I—"

"*Tofurky*," she hissed. "You're the guy who makes the tofu turkey?"

She didn't wait for an answer.

"I thought it was a *joke*, but people just keep calling me from all over the country wanting to know about this damned tofu turkey of yours. I almost had to change my number!"

"I'm sorry about that," I said. "I meant no harm. How about if I send you a free Tofurky so you can see what all the calls are about?"

"A free tofu turkey? What in the world would I do with a damned *tofu turkey*? I am sick to death of tofu turkeys. I think your company sucks. I think you suck. I just want these damned vegetarians to stop calling my salon!"

She went on for another five minutes, and I listened patiently until her anger was more or less spent. I felt bad for all the calls she was getting because of my creative spelling. At the same time, I was glad to have solved the mystery.

As 1996 came to a close, we had sold 1,500 Tofurkys, nearly doubling sales from the previous year. Three hundred of those were directly via Dave's Simple Living Network from phone and online orders. Pizza Hut claims that it sold a pepperoni pizza online in 1994, but Dave's Tofurky sales from his house in tiny Trout Lake, Washington, were the real pioneers for internet food sales.

Doubling our sales still didn't make us a lot of money, but it was more growth than I'd ever seen from my well-behaved tempeh products, and that made me look forward to the next time around.

The Breakthrough

As I sorted through our 1996 feedback cards, the message was the same as from the year before. They loved the concept, appreciated our efforts, but wanted something cheaper, smaller, and with a more appealing texture. They were also interested in a roast that had the stuffing inside. That was good feedback, but we weren't sure how to give our growing customer base what they wanted. Even if you bake it, tofu just doesn't freeze well. On top of that, the baked tofu for the 1996 Tofurky didn't look nearly as good as Hans's 1995 stuffed roast. It was just a slab. So we added that to our list of goals for the 1997 Tofurky—create something that was a feast for the eyes as well as the stomach.

Early in 1997, a vegan pioneer named Mark visited Turtle Island. Mark had run a company called Meat of Wheat, which sold products made from seitan. Seitan is made from wheat gluten and is an excellent source of protein. It works well as a vegetarian stand-in for meat in lots of recipes because the texture is very meaty. In spite of his best efforts, Mark's company hadn't made it, but along the way, he had discovered a way to use seitan to make stuffed holiday roasts.

He pulled out one of his roasts, and it was beautiful. It was a compact, twenty-six-ounce roast with an outer shell made from seitan and breadcrumb stuffing on the inside. He used one food extruder to first create the outer shell and a second to push the stuffing into the middle. We cooked one up there in the Turtle Island break room, and it was delicious.

"These look great," I told Mark, "but do you think you could add tofu to the recipe?"

If this was going to be the next Tofurky, it needed tofu.

"We can try," he said, "but it might mess with the texture."

That was okay with me. The texture on Mark's roast was the only thing I didn't care for. It was a little too heavy. I thought that the tofu might lighten things up a little.

Two weeks later, Mark brought in a sample roast made with tofu. When we cooked it up, we both thought the taste and texture were great. I was excited. Turtle Island was still too small and unprofitable to have its own research and development team, so all the recipe development had to be outsourced. In this case, the Tofurky solution walked through the door and found me. It felt like a benevolent universe sending me a gift, possibly as a make-up call for all those years in the tempeh mines.

There was just one tiny catch. After Meat of Wheat went out of business, Mark licensed the recipe to a tamale maker in Chico, California. She was using it as faux chicken in some of her tamales but not in any big volume. So I reached out to the tamale maker, Karen, and she agreed to make these new Tofurky roasts in Chico and ship them to Hood River for us to assemble and distribute to our growing collection of wholesalers. That worked out too. Turtle Island was still mostly a tempeh company and didn't have the equipment to make these new roasts. Co-packing was a great way to start.

Karen turned out to be a great partner. She set up her equipment to mix the ingredients and extrude each roast and then its inner stuffing into ham nettings. That made the roasts look even better. Karen's system also made the product scalable. Without relying on a lot of expensive labor, she could produce up to 1,000 Tofurkys in an eight-hour shift. We agreed on a price, and then I added enough marketing margin that there was a slim chance we might actually make a profit on this year's Tofurky. In August, I placed an order for 15,000 Tofurky roasts, with shipments to be delivered on four different dates from the end of September to December.

To finance this holiday investment, Turtle Island needed a line of credit of $160,000, which was about a third of our gross annual sales for 1996—a big chunk of money for our modest operation. It was a high-risk bet on a product that had only sold 1,500 units the year before and hadn't yet become profitable. Because Turtle Island was taking on all of the risk and would no longer be paying Higher Taste to produce the roasts with this new recipe, Hans and Rhonda dropped out at this point, but they would soon be back to play another important role in Tofurky history.

Mark's new recipe and Karen's tamale shop solved all of the problems our customers had pointed out. The taste and texture were now just right. Tofurkys looked great too, and could even be carved up and placed attractively in the center of the table. We packed the 1997 Tofurkys in a smaller box, about the size of a shoebox. The feast included one twenty-six-ounce Tofurky roast, four tempeh drummettes, and fifteen ounces of Tofurky gravy. The list price was $23.95, but we sold it for a more affordable $19.95 in a holiday promotion.

To market the product, we still sent out the usual press releases and in-store materials, but those efforts were small compared to the free press we were receiving. By 1997, Tofurky had become part of the national conversation thanks to our unpaid marketing department, the national media. Tofurky showed up on ABC's *Good Morning America*, CNBC's *Steals and Deals*, and local TV news shows across the country. The *Los Angeles Times* and *Washington Post* carried favorable reviews. On *The Tonight Show*, actress Christina Applegate told Jay Leno that she had enjoyed a Tofurky at Thanksgiving. The media coverage all came to us spontaneously, without any help from PR agencies. Part of that coverage was probably due to the media becoming more aware of the vegetarian segment of society, but I also think that part of it was due to how much fun it was to say the word "Tofurky."

The free advertising happened in smaller conversations too. I went to more than one party that fall and overheard people I didn't know talking about Tofurky around the beer keg. I'm sure those weren't the only parties in America where our product was discussed. Tofurky went viral in the old-school way by moving from person to person by word of mouth. It was a remarkable product, and people were remarking on it. Even in this third year of the unruly product child's life, it was starting to become a sign of the changing times. Vegans, vegetarians, and meat reducers now had a place at the table. And what did you serve them? Tofurky.

Distribution improved a lot that year. We were able to serve markets across most of the US. We again sold Tofurkys for $49.95 through the Simple Living Network, but with more people finding twenty-dollar Tofurkys in their local natural food stores and co-ops, the online sales were much smaller. People were willing to drive for hours to find their Tofurky in person.

Sales took off. We didn't have any trouble selling all 15,000 of the Tofurkys we ordered from Karen's shop. In fact, we had to order extra roasts to meet the Christmas demand. By the end of the year, we sold 18,000 Tofurkys—twelve times the amount we sold in 1996. Even more striking, though, was that Tofurky accounted for forty percent of Turtle Island's annual sales. We tripled our annual gross sales in just three years.

The feedback we received that year was the best yet. Many people commented on the improved texture and taste, and several told us they were happy to see that the holiday roast once again looked "pretty," like Hans's first Tofurky. The public demand that fall also caused natural food wholesalers and even a few forward-thinking supermarkets to reach out to us about making sure they would have a good supply of the now fame-*ish* Tofurky for the next year's holidays.

By 1997, I was a smart enough businessman to know that there is no such thing as smooth sailing in the food industry. I knew I was on a path that moved from one problem to the next—and also that the point isn't to not have problems, either. The point is to keep solving your problems in creative ways so that you can keep moving in the right direction.

Tofurky Feast Boxes, 1997 to 1999. Notice that the Tofurky Feast is now described as "vegan" compared to the 1995 edition, which used the word "vegetarian."
(Turtle Island Foods, Inc.)

I remember sitting at the kitchen table with Sue on New Year's Eve. Luke had finally gone to sleep. We were exhausted from trying to get him to sleep but mostly from having endured the most intense fall on record. But we were so happy too. We could see that we were moving in the right direction with Tofurky, that this product was going to take us to a lot of new and exciting places. Sue lifted her glass of champagne. I clinked it. And then we went to bed well before midnight because—I may have already mentioned this—we were exhausted.

Making the Most of the Moment

We weren't finished with this unruly product child in 1997. The Tofurky brand had established an initial beachhead with the US natural foods consumer—and beyond—thanks entirely to our flagship product, the Tofurky Feast. Turtle Island had changed from a West Coast company to a national brand. All the sales brokers who used to ignore our tempeh were now calling me up every week to talk Tofurky.

As promising as this was, it was also dangerous because we'd become heavily dependent on a single product. If something happened to prevent us from producing Tofurkys, or if a strong competitor arrived on the scene, we'd be toast. It could take the whole company down. It was also not great to depend so heavily on the fourth quarter to make it through the rest of the year. Fortunately, a strategy for how to diversify was easy to find by examining the meat-based protein industry we were starting to disrupt. How did the turkey industry survive outside of the holidays? They put their turkeys into sandwiches in the form of thin, round slices.

So that's what we did, starting early in 1998. I called Karen, our Tofurky co-packer, and had her send me some logs of Tofurky

Tofurky Deli Slice ad from 1998. These were groundbreaking products at the time and came in Original, Hickory Smoked, and Peppered flavors. They are still top sellers and dominate the plant-based deli subcategory. *(Turtle Island Foods, Inc.)*

without the Holiday Feast stuffing in them. Then I borrowed a counter-top meat slicer from a guy who ran a butcher shop supplier in Portland.

"Make sure you cut it paper thin," he said. "That makes the best sandwiches. Very tasty."

"Also," he said, "don't cut your fingers off. This is a very sharp piece of equipment."

Back at Turtle Island, I put a log of Tofurky onto the slicer, being very careful to not cut my fingers off. The Tofurky sliced beautifully, paper thin. It tasted great. The texture was right. From the first bite of that sandwich, I could see us getting the product into stores right away.

The only thing that worried me was that a single product would get lost on the shelves. I asked Karen if she could add some whole peppercorns to the mix. That was not a problem, so we had a second flavor—peppered. Then I put a Tofurky log into a small smoker from home and fired it up outside on the loading dock. After about half an hour, the hickory chips had done their work, adding beautiful light-brown crust to the Tofurky. That sandwich was even tastier than the original. So there we were with three new deli products to take to market—original, hickory smoked, and peppered deli slices.

Tofurky Deli Slices were a hit right from the start. Between the new line of deli slices, another big year for Tofurky Feasts, and the steady growth of tempeh, we had over a million dollars in gross sales in 1998. That was something I'd never really imagined was possible, even when I was counting on tempeh to be the next granola. Most surprising of all was that after eighteen years in business, there was money left over. We made our first profit. It wasn't a rags-to-riches story yet, but it was definitely rags to better rags.

Our next effort at making the most of our Tofurky moment was to expand to Great Britain. Selling in the UK was great as a fun fact to drop into conversation with reporters. Selling on two continents gave some credibility to the brand. However, the hassle of jumping through all the export hoops was making the lives of our front-office staff borderline miserable. We had four people managing the company back then. The extra stress of working the UK market diverted their attention from all of the easier opportunities for expansion within the US. Landing one big supermarket chain could easily match the annual sales of the entire UK market—and we wouldn't have to change "flavor" to "flavour" on every package. After two years, we gave it up—for the time being.

Turtle Island's failed attempt at global domination was not entirely a failure, however. Like most of my failures, it taught me a valuable lesson. After many visits to natural foods stores in the UK and Europe, I noticed that veggie burgers were not a big deal on the other side of the Atlantic. In Europe, it was all about sausages—Italian sausage, kielbasa, brats, Lincolnshire, and many other flavors. That gave me an idea. What if we made Tofurky sausages? Would Tofurky sausages sell in the burger-obsessed US market?

I went to several Whole Foods stores to survey the landscape. In every store, I counted at least nine brands of tofu or soy-protein hot dogs—small ones, long ones, chilidogs, and more. It was clear that there was plenty of demand for plant-based alternatives to non-burger grill items. However, did the US market really need to have nine different versions of the same basic flavor? I didn't think so. It seemed to me that there was room for something different to put on the grill—Tofurky sausage, which as I may have already mentioned, did not yet exist.

We still didn't have any full-time research and development team, so I called up my old friend and former Tofurky partner, Hans. Would he be interested in creating three new sausage flavors for us? Hans said yes, so we set up a royalty contract that gave Hans a percentage of sales revenue for five years, at which time his recipes would become ours. This revenue ended up being in the mid-six-figure range for what amounted to just three months of part-time development work, but it was well worth it for us. Working with Hans, we were able to quickly bring out three different sausages: beer brat, Italian, and kielbasa.

We launched Tofurky sausages just in time for Memorial Day, the start of summer grilling season, and they were an instant hit. Once again, we'd found an underserved niche—the summer grill. For years, vegans had been left out of the barbecue season just like they'd been left out of Thanksgiving. Tofurky sausages brought a new demographic to the outdoor grill and breathed new life into the refrigerated, meat-free hot dog shelf. It was also easy for food brokers to pull out three of those nine brands of hot dogs and replace them with these big dogs that offered new and exciting flavors. The sausages were a ground-breaking hit back then, and today they've become a category of their own—a must-have for any brand.

The third thing we did to change the business and set us on the path we're on now was to stop relying on co-packers and instead bring all of our production in-house. That meant buying the rights to Mark's seitan roast recipe and expanding our Hood River operation to handle all of the Tofurky production that Karen had been doing for us in Chico.

This was a long and complicated process that is pretty interesting if you're in the food business—we were the first to adapt the double-extruder to the vegan roast market, for example—and not as interesting if you aren't. For this book, bringing the production in-house is important mostly because it marked the moment when we stopped being a bootstrap operation and instead funded our growth in more conventional ways. I fired myself from doing sales and hired a marketing director, Mark, to live and breathe sales, which he did way better than I did. We took over the the entire 26,000-square-foot building we'd leased in Hood River—and later bought it. We started getting calls from venture capitalists looking for a piece of the action. Once we found the wild Tofurky and built it into a brand, this became a different kind of business story. That other story is a whole book by itself, in other words, so it will have to wait for another time, or possibly never.

Final Jeopardy

Turtle Island moved into the new century with a strong line of Tofurky products—holiday roasts, deli slices, jurky, and sausages. These lines all became industry leaders in a growing alternative proteins market that Turtle Island had been faithfully pioneering for twenty years. Total sales in the new century were split pretty evenly—one-third holiday Tofurky products, one-third everyday Tofurky products, and one-third tempeh products. Good old tempeh!

It wasn't until fall of 2002, however, that I *knew* I'd finally made it as a businessman. I was sitting at my desk about to call it a day when the phone rang. It was my Aunt Rosie from Minneapolis. This is the same Aunt Rosie who twenty years earlier had sat me down after a fine holiday meal and told me unequivocally that trying to sell soybeans to the meat-eating American public was a stupid idea. She was excited.

"Seth!" she said.

"Aunt Rosie."

"Seth!"

"It's good to hear from you."

"Seth," she said. "I just had to call."

Then Aunt Rosie took a deep breath and in measured sentences told me that she had been watching *Jeopardy!* on her television, just like she always does. Someone chose something for $400, and the answer was "Thanksgiving alternative created by entrepreneur Seth Tibbott."

"What is Tofurky?" I ventured. She paid that no attention.

"You were on *Jeopardy!*," she said. "*Jeopardy!*"

Aunt Rosie wasn't calling to say that maybe I had been right about soybeans after all, but *her* excitement over my success made *me* excited about our success. I still think of Aunt Rosie's phone call as the moment when the long, bootstrapping, learning-from-mistakes phase of my business life came to a satisfying conclusion. Because I was on *Jeopardy!* Tofurky was a part of the landscape.

20/20 HINDSIGHT:
Sometimes You Just Know

Pivoting towards Tofurky was a great, life-changing moment for Turtle Island. After years of struggle, happy and otherwise, the joy of that almost unexpected success was overwhelming. I can't tell you how much *fun* it was to see my ship finally come in.

And my story is not all that unique. A lot of businesses have started out with one can't-miss product or idea as their north star without much success before pivoting to follow a new product on a new and successful course. Sometimes these pivots are just a small tweak to the original dream. YouTube started out as an online dating site that asked people to post videos of their perfect partner. They literally couldn't *pay* people to sign up. But when the YouTube founders discovered the bigger market in silly and informational videos, the brand took off. Starbucks originally sold coffee beans and espresso machines, but after a visit to Italy, Howard Schultz saw the value in coffee shops. And that was that.

But how can you tell if the pivot you have in mind is going to be your big moment or just another bad guess? How can you tell the difference between a Tofurky moment and a Keep It Simple Stirfry moment? The general answer is that you can't tell in advance. You can only tell from the results. If it changes everything, then you know it was a turning point, a great pivot. If it doesn't make it big—or if it fails miserably—then you perform the usual business autopsy to gather lessons from your mistakes, and you move on.

However, that's not quite the full answer. You can also sometimes tell that it's going to be big because you just know it. Remember Al Jacobson and his blue corn chips? He just knew in his gut that they were going to be a big hit, and they were. How did he know? I don't think it was magic. I think it was a finely tuned intuition that told him. He'd been in the business for a long time. He'd had a lot of success and a lot of failure. And when he dreamed up blue corn chips, all that experience helped him to see a winner from deep in his gut. He just knew it.

My big pivot from tempeh to Tofurky almost didn't happen because I was still learning to trust my own finely tuned business intuition. Those fifteen years of losing money had eroded my business confidence, but under the surface they had also sharpened my business intuition. So even as I was starting to think that I just wasn't cut out for business, my intuition was telling me that this was it, the big moment, the time to use that word I'd been carrying around for so long, Tofurky, and bring something new to market. I really struggled with whether to trust my intuition or go along with all the reasonable voices that said it was a mistake. There was no data to suggest that turkey-flavored tofu for Thanksgiving would be the next big thing. But intuition won out, and now here we are.

If you've been following your path diligently and creatively and it's still not working, you might be a lot closer to success than you think. That whole "darkest hour before the dawn" mantra has some weight to it for the bootstrapper. Sometimes the only thing standing between you and success is adding one more seemingly unimportant piece to the puzzle. Sometimes it's taking everything you've learned with one product and using it with another one. That's the thing about the big moment—you can't ever tell when it's going to come. You just have to prepare for it as well as you can and then go for it when your intuition tells you it's time.

THE TOFURKY COMPANY

Moving into the Present

The ancient Greeks have two words for time. *Chronos* was their word for sequential or chronological time. *Kairos* was their word for an all-encompassing, supreme moment when time seems to stand still and you can finally see your path forward. Chronos stresses you out as you plod along. Kairos refreshes you with long-awaited insight.

In this story, the chronos time zone was the bootstrapping phase—all those years of living on nothing and slowly, slowly growing the business into something that at least resembled a business, even if it wasn't making money. Our kairos time zone was the Tofurky moment—especially when we went from 1,500 to 18,000 Tofurky roasts in 1997 but also as we built our lines of everyday Tofurky products like deli slices, sausages, and chick'n. That's where we saw our path forward after years of hacking our way through the forest.

In 1998, Turtle Island hit a million dollars in gross sales and—believe it or not—turned a small profit. We paid off Bob's big loan from 1992. We still had some chronos-style mop-up to do as we built our production shop, expanded sales, hired more staff, and brought in new and better equipment. But we weren't really bootstrapping anymore because now we had become a fully launched brand. Bankers liked us. Brokers and retailers started contacting us for a change. Even our tax guy quit making fun of me, at least to my face. In fact, it was a big moment when he finally said, "Dude, this business is too complicated for me. You need to go to Portland and hire some experts."

The Tofurky moment had turned us around, and it didn't really stop once we turned around, either. Tofurky madness became an annual fall event for the media and holiday shoppers. The buzz around Tofurky was like no other vegan product in history. It just got louder every year. Customers sent us letters and emails every winter that were almost all thank you notes, with a few love letters mixed in. Here's one example:

This was my first vegan Thanksgiving. I bought a Tofurky Feast, even though I was sticker-shocked at the $25.00 retail price. I grumbled a bit but took it home anyway. On Thanksgiving, I took it to my Mom's house, surrounded by my family of omnivores. I prepared the Feast and put it on the table next to the turkey. I had to fight with my relatives to get a second serving. Several said if they could eat food like this every day, they would give up meat as I have.

—Jane in Dayton, Ohio

Here's another example:

Having been a vegetarian since 1975, I've always been on the lookout for fun, delicious food around the holidays. I brought my Tofurky to a traditional feast today and every-

one was quite curious. Most had never considered the idea of a meat substitute and assumed that it would be bland and mushy. To my delight, it was absolutely terrific! I am looking forward to Tofurky sandwiches tomorrow!

—*Bill in Atlanta, Georgia*

It was *so* satisfying to hear that kind of praise after all my years of working in obscurity, just barely keeping the dream alive, and making mistake after mistake after mistake. The business success was great, of course, but it was mostly a great relief, especially at first. It was a relief to finally be able to support my little family, to see Bob rewarded for his years of generous investment in Turtle Island, to have something tangible to show for my twenty years of bootstrapping with plant-based proteins. The praise we got from customers was different. It was satisfying because our products made people's lives better. It was a sweet validation of the mission behind the business, an affirmation that all those years of bootstrapping were worth it on a karmic level.

Looking back at the story, it's been fascinating—for me, anyway—to see how our core values developed so naturally in those long years spent learning from mistakes. What I've noticed is that those core values that brought us to our Tofurky moment are still the core values that guide The Tofurky Company. They are our secret sauce, a sauce that simmered over the low flames of those first eighteen years in business.

I'll end the story by giving you the ingredients to our secret sauce. You should be able to improve upon our recipe with your own business. You'll just have to figure out your quantities and simmer it over your own flames.

Treat People Well

Over the years, I did all the jobs from production to sales to office work to mopping floors. What I learned is that it takes a lot of hard work from a lot of different people to make good food day in and day out. The jobs are all hard, with their own unique kinds of stress, and it's wrong to pretend that one person's headaches from managing the sales are significantly worse than someone else's headaches from keeping the floors and bathrooms clean in a production shop. They're just different. Doing all the jobs myself gave me a higher level of empathy for the headaches of others and deep gratitude for the hard work and dedication of all my employees.

Today, the new CEO, my stepson Jaime Athos, and his management team have expanded on this promise and made The Tofurky Company a Certified B Corporation, otherwise known as a "B Corp." The "B" is for "benefit." B Corps are legally required to consider the impact of their decisions on their workers, customers, suppliers, community, and the environment—not just shareholders. B Corps promise:

- We must be the change we seek in the world.
- All business ought to be conducted as if people and places mattered.
- Through their products, practices, and profits, businesses should aspire to do no harm and benefit all.
- To do so requires that we act with the understanding that we are each dependent upon one another and thus responsible for each other and future generations.

During those lean bootstrap years, our main public benefit was to blaze a trail for others to follow in the meat alternative business. The small market and my even smaller understanding of business meant there was never enough money around to benefit our employees with the wages and benefits they deserved. It was a great day when we were finally able to pay for our employees' insurance and retirement plans many years ago. Becoming a B Corp takes our commitment to our employees and this community even further.

Having lived through long years of waiting for the phone to ring, I also learned to value my customers because I had so few of them. I did everything I could to make things pleasant and ultimately satisfying for the retailers, distributors, and consumers

Tofurky Roast with caramelized onions and cherries, 2019. Served on over five million tables. *(Turtle Island Foods, Inc.)*

who did call. That's another way to treat your people well, and it continues to be an important value.

We now ship out hundreds of thousands of packages of Tofurky and Tempeh every week of the year. We try to be perfect, but you've read the story, so you know that mistakes are just a normal part of business, a pathway to less stupidity and greater competence. We still make them. When a complaint comes in—from anyone—we take it very seriously. First off, we always own the mistake and apologize for its impact on the customer. Second, we go the extra mile to make things right. We don't just fix what was broken, but toss in something extra in thanks for the time they've taken to reach out to us. And third, we track every complaint and use them to fine-tune our systems and lower the chance of future screw-ups.

Don't Take Yourself Too Seriously

One secret-sauce ingredient that keeps on showing up, not just in my business life but my *life* life, is that I try to keep things fun for everyone—customers, employees, vendors, reporters, and anyone else who crosses paths with a Tofurky. British writer and philosopher G. K. Chesterton said: "angels can fly because they can take themselves lightly." I think the same applies to Tofurkys, even though they have leaves instead of wings.

I picked up my love for fun at an early age from my dad and his penguin-themed creations. My mom always tried to make any birthday or gathering magical too, with costumes and skits and other little tricks she had for turning an ordinary event into something more fun than it had any right to be. And I just kept up their good work in college—with the Free School and working at the Glen—and for years and years as a wandering naturalist.

One time I put a scarecrow in a lawn chair in the middle of a collection of bird feeders. I put a small tray of seed right on the scarecrow's lap. After the birds got used to the scarecrow, I took the rowdiest kids in camp that week, dressed them in the scarecrow's jacket, and sat them in the chair with a tray of birdseed. They had never sat so still during the entire week, and the rest of the class had never been so silent as they were when a little song sparrow landed in their lap. You don't get moments like that if you aren't trying to have fun.

From the first days of Turtle Island, we also tried to have some fun with this weird product that nobody had ever heard of. We created "Tempehroni," as you've seen, with a soybean character throwing a pizza on the label. My friend Jan did the drawings for that label, the Turtle Island logo, and other fun marketing materials.

In the bootstrapping workplace, we also tried to keep things light, especially in the early days when we had a limited ability to pay people. Employees spend so much of their lives with us that

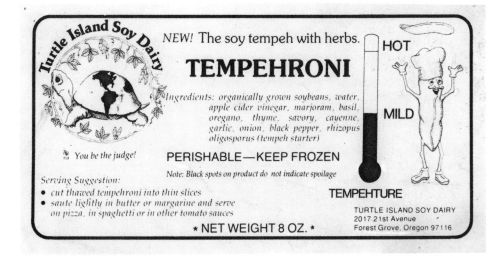

The original packaging for my Tempehroni "sausage." (Turtle Island Foods, Inc.)

we try to inject fun wherever possible. We shut down the tempeh line to hang out by or in the White Salmon River when attitudes needed adjustment. Pick-up basketball and parties in the gym helped to ease the aches and pains of tempeh production and kept the operation from becoming too serious.

The creation of the Tofurky brand in 1995 brought that light-heartedness back into our marketing but now it played a starring role. I was betting that customers were going to enjoy the name of the product as much as the product. As one TV reporter put it, "Who can say the name 'Tofurky' without smiling?"

Humor became such an obvious company value that it served as sort of a litmus test for prospective vendors. The salesman who came up to sell us $500,000 mixers dressed as a riverboat gambler had us at "hello." A refrigeration repairman dressed up as the Easter Bunny and jogged through the office giving out candy. We invited him back too.

It's always been a bit of a tightrope walk to have such a serious product, a product that we hope will change the way people get their protein, with such a funny name. It opened us up for criticism and a lot of eye-rolling, but overall, it's been a positive. Sometimes the passion runs so deep with vegans, or anyone who's deeply committed to a cause, that they come off as holier than thou to others. The lightheartedness embedded in the Tofurky name helps the product to be serious without taking itself too seriously.

Work the Media

Tofurky got a massive amount of free media attention right from the start. That attention helped to spotlight the whole category of vegan and natural foods like no other brand had ever done.

What's amazing is that all of the early attention came during the days of "unsocial media," when you had to fight with much bigger brands for television airtime. In the first ten years of the Tofurky brand's life, we spent next to nothing on public relations. We didn't need to. In the first twenty years of Tofurky, we spent less than $20,000 on hired public relations. Today, new brands will likely spend $20,000 on public relations in a single *month*.

For the first ten years of the Tofurky brand's life, it showed up in all the major US newspapers, on four Food Network episodes, on all the morning and late-night talk shows, in radio interviews, and on local and national nightly news broadcasts many times. As impressive as that is, what made the brand such a cultural icon was all the times it showed up in the mouths of fictional characters:

- A zombie actor on *The X-Files* spits out the "flesh" he had bitten out of a woman's shoulder because it was actually turkey and not Tofurky. "I asked for Tofurky, not turkey! Half the zombies are vegetarians," he whines as he runs off stage in horror.
- Lisa Simpson asks for Tofurky for Thanksgiving on *The Simpsons*.
- On NBC's *Just Shoot Me*, a woman tells her husband to "be a man and go get some Tofurky."
- An ad for Grand Marnier asks, "What would the founding fathers think of Tofurky?"
- An episode of ABC's *Felicity* ends with everyone sitting around a table raising a glass "to Tofurky."

And that's just a small sampling. Tofurky found its way onto *Oprah*, *The Colbert Report*, *Jeopardy!*, Tofurky hunting and Tofurky raising sketches on *Conan*, and many other shows. It still shows up on TV all the time.

That exposure, as much as anything else, helped the brand to catch fire quickly. When you see a retail product in a movie—like Reese's Pieces in *E.T.*—you can almost always be sure that the brand paid for that product placement. Those placements usually *start* at $10,000. But we've never paid a penny for any of Tofurky's appearances. It's like Tofurky has become short-hand for writers. If a character has Tofurky in the fridge, it tells the audience something about the character.

In the early years of Tofurky, it was pretty easy to work the media because they came flocking to us. The month of November became pretty stressful, trying to deal with all the media attention and demands. There was a moment when I put a reporter from the *New York Times* on hold so I could take a call from the *Washington Post*. That was pretty fun, but more importantly, it was instructive. Okay, I thought, *that's* not going to happen again. And then—here's the instructive part—I realized that if we wanted to keep getting all the free media attention, which we did, we might want to start working a little harder to keep the interest up by giving the media new stories to report about Tofurky.

The first of these stories arose from a *Wall Street Journal* article in November 1998, "Tofurky: Vegetarian Nirvana." The article began with this question:

> *The big question is: What does a Tofurky look like? Until we establish that, our nation's schoolchildren will be hobbled, unable to draw Tofurkys or piece them together with colorful construction paper cutouts.*

The writer had a point. Though we knew what our creation looked like on the table, we had no knowledge of what they looked like in the wild. In 1999, we decided to give back to the media by responding to this question with a "Draw the Tofurky in the Wild" contest. We offered a prize of a free trip to the World Headquarters of the Tofurky Empire in Hood River, Oregon. Then we printed posters and sent them to stores across the US. I called up the *Wall Street Journal* reporter who had written the article in the first place and invited her to be a judge. She graciously accepted.

That fall, hundreds of entries came flooding in. Kids, teens, moms—along with actual graphic artists—all sent in their renditions. They were all great fun, but most of them had one serious problem—they had heads, legs, and wings like turkey turkeys. The winner was one of only two plant-based entries. In her winning entry, she even included a poem about how Tofurky Roasts grew on trees and fell to the ground in the fall. Of course! There *was* a faint hint of a face on the winning Tofurky-in-the-wild drawing, but we passed that off as unintentional, like the potato chips people find that resemble Abraham Lincoln. That year, our *WSJ* judge chronicled this contest in a second article. Another fun contest was the "Travels with Tofurky," which asked customers to send in photos of themselves and a Tofurky from their travels.

Since then, we've done our part to seed the media with new products, new contests, and press releases that track the number of total roasts sold, which is something reporters always want to know. In 2006, as we approached the one millionth Tofurky Roast, we held a contest to see who could guess closest to the exact number of roasts that would be sold by the end of that year. Out of the more than four thousand who entered for the chance to win an electric scooter, my old girlfriend Rhonda—the same Rhonda who helped me make my first batch of tempeh in Tennessee in 1977—was one of the top five finalists. She was a math teacher, so it made perfect sense, even though she had no inside

"Travels with Tofurky" contest winner Carl Lambert, freefalling with his Tofurky feast high above Orange, Virginia, 2009. *(Turtle Island Foods, Inc.)*

information, I swear. However, I was relieved when another woman won the contest by guessing 1,083,526, which was only 108 Tofurkys less than the actual number sold.

I always thought that the media would eventually get tired of telling and retelling the Tofurky story. But after twenty-five years, it hasn't gotten tired yet. Reporters keep calling, and Tofurky keeps showing up on late-night TV, in movies, in interviews, and on TV shows.

Follow the Mission

The Tofurky Company has always stayed true to my original, pie-in-the-sky-dreamer mission of bringing tasty, low-on-the-food-chain, plant-based foods to the world. That mission has grown over the years to include support for animal rights and environmental protection. It continues to be right at the heart of what we do here.

Today, this is our vision and mission:

- Vision: To help create a world where animals aren't used for food, and people are satiated, healthy, and content.
- Mission: To lead people toward plant-based foods by offering enticing alternatives to their current diets that make their transition seamless and enduring.

To further advance our environmental mission, we now produce our Tofurky products in a new Hood River factory that we built to the highest environmental standards possible. It features 400 solar panels, free electric car charging, and a green roof that is over forty percent more efficient than Oregon Building codes require.

The Tofurky Company headquarters in Hood River, Oregon, 2018. *(Wes Braun)*

Keep Your Equity

Today we make more than thirty-five Tofurky and tempeh products, all of which are 100% vegan and always have been. We sell
these products on six continents and in over 27,000 stores. That's
amazing, right? What's even more amazing is that in spite of this
wild growth, we are still family owned and independent. We've
never sold any of our equity to anyone outside of the family.

Keeping our equity was originally—and for all of the bootstrap
years—a matter of necessity. The only investors I had access to
were my brother Bob and my mom. Once we had our Tofurky
moment, we had plenty of offers from investors, but by then they
were too late. Keeping our equity in the company meant that we
could run it the way we wanted to run it—following our mission,
having fun along the way, and taking care of our people. Once
you start selling your equity, you invite more stakeholders into the

214

business and slowly turn yourself into their employee rather than staying your own boss.

In September 2014, after thirty-five years as Grand Poobah and President, I handed the management of The Tofurky Company over to my very capable stepson, Jaime Athos. Jaime has continued the mission of Tofurky and taken it places I never dreamed of. I'm trying to retire, but it's not going very well. I continue to help expand the Tofurky brand throughout the world, and I volunteer my time to work with nonprofits that support animal rights, environmental protection, and promoting a plant-based diet.

Moving into the Future

I'm so proud of this company that my family and employees have helped me build. I'm also honored that somehow a benevolent universe nudged me toward pioneering the plant-based protein industry that is exploding today.

Each night after work—or retirement, I guess, which still looks a lot like work—I drive home from the shiny, eco-friendly Tofurky Headquarters in Hood River, cross the Columbia River, and head north to wait for a minute at Klickitat County's only stop light before heading up to my home in Trout Lake.

Highway 141 follows the frothy White Salmon, which has now been designated an official National Wild and Scenic River. Ten miles upstream, the road gently dips into the now bustling town of Husum. All summer long and into the fall, my once-quiet tempeh town is crammed with rafters and kayakers from Portland. Don and Betty's Café is now run by a rafting company, and it serves espresso, craft beer, and kombucha.

In the old elementary school, four shiny fire trucks fill the bays that were built into the classrooms that used to house piano-tuning

Hood River, Oregon (2018; population: 7,990) as seen from across the Columbia River. Tofurky's old and new plants can be seen in the foreground, and Mt. Hood (11,250 ft.) in the background. *(Sue Tibbott)*

clowns, Mom and Pop gift boxes, and my little office/warehouse. The tiny kitchen, my tempeh Nirvana from 1981 that produced all those thousands of tons of tempeh for more than a decade, is still intact but mostly sits idle. Another mile up the highway and off to the west, my treehouse is still up in the trees, but it's now a sanctuary for squirrels, flying and otherwise.

My dad, the penguin artist, was born in 1896 and thus saw a lot of change in his eighty-two years, from the Wright Brothers' flight at Fort Myer, Virginia, in 1908 to the first footprints on the moon in 1969. I'm starting to understand what that feels like. It's breathtaking for me to see all the changes in the natural foods market since I first started delivering my tempeh to stores throughout Portland in my beat-up, "some body damage" Datsun wagon.

More and more brands are jumping into this market and making lots of noise as millions of people move toward healthier, sustainable, and compassionate plant-based diets. Good for them. And bootstrapper, if that's what you have in mind, good for you. It's a big job veganizing the world's diet, and we need all hands on deck. After all the change I've seen in the last couple of decades, it suddenly feels within reach for me to see this world shift from the present where people get most of their meat and dairy from animals to a future where they get most, or all, of their meat and dairy from plants. It has been a great joy of my life to have played a small part in helping this better world come into view. It's coming hard and fast now. I can feel it.

ACKNOWLEDGMENTS

How does one thank and acknowledge a lifetime of support, kindness, and generosity that helped bring The Tofurky Company to life? It's a daunting and nearly impossible task. Please know that any person who has ever worked here for one day is honored and appreciated along with many other supporters. But deserving particular note in rough order of appearance are:

Betty and Lloyd Tibbott and my Uncle John Lundquist, for passing down humor, positivity, and kindness.

My brother Bob, for unwavering support financially and spiritually.

Doug Dickensen and Glen Helen Outdoor Center, for taking a chance on a college dropout.

Tony Russell, for his vision and compassion for all humans.

Laurel McKowen, for being years ahead of her time and cooking a great meal of lentils, rice, and onions.

ACKNOWLEDGMENTS

Stephen Gaskin and the Farm, for their tireless work bringing tempeh and cutting-edge vegan products to the world before they were a glint in the eye of any US supermarkets.

Bill and Katy McKinney, for turning my head around on the value of small business and teaching me that "from the roots of esoterism flowers banality."

Debbie Henry, for intuitive tempeh cooking skills, vivid memories, and writing skills.

Jan Muir, for donating an incredible logo, catchy drawings, and ads before I even realized I was supposed to be paying for them. Not that I could have at the time, but still . . .

Belinda Hanley and family, for being the first supporters in the world of this crazy dream.

Robert Grott and the Hope Co-op, for business wisdom and incredible generosity. Sorry I almost burnt the place to the ground. All good now?

Alexander Lyon and family, for bringing tempeh from the labs of Cornell and the NRRL in Peoria, IL.

Jimmy Carter, for all the eco-friendly federal programs that led me to amass $7,500 in 1980.

Ronald Reagan, for taking away all my eco-friendly jobs and forcing me to pivot.

Rick Melching, for seeing the wisdom in renting the Husum School to a nobody.

Margret Walker, for pushing the Husum School rental forward and for years of community service.

Chuck Williams, for a life of environmental activism in the Columbia Gorge and White Salmon Valley.

Amber Yezek, for friendship, hard work, and being a fair tree-house landlord.

Sue Hall and family, for friendship and helping save the wild habitats of the Columbia Gorge.

Luther Olsen, for all those thousands of gallons of water at a price even a starving tempeh-maker could afford.

Dick and Bonnie Smith, for their extreme generosity of a free, clean apartment that didn't smell of mouse urine and had both heat and a warm shower.

Ace and Space, clowns who brought joy and ambiance to the tempeh experience.

Bart and Roma Barton, stand-up people, surrogate parents, and great woodworkers.

Sycamore Associates, for being A+ renters and even better friends and people.

ACKNOWLEDGMENTS

Ken Williams, for many free nights in Portland and resale of short dated tempeh products.

Charlie Hyman, for his good heart and soft couch before I had a couch of my own.

Rhonda Frick Wright, for good soybean splitting skills and help getting this crazy tempeh dream off the ground.

Jim Wells, for his sense of humor, adventure, discovery of the White Salmon River Valley, and for hiring his well-qualified naturalist friends.

Sue Tibbott, for love, friendship, Tofu Key Lime pies, tremendous bookkeeping skills, and creating two incredible sons.

Luke Tibbott, for giving daily inspiration to work hard and create a world he can be proud of.

Dave Wampler, for his early vision of the power of the internet and for bringing organization to a most disorganized office.

Hans and Rhonda Wrobel, for their ground-breaking work on Tofurky and in advancing veganism with their amazing cooking skills.

Graciela Pulido, for tirelessly working to provide an example of what a manager should be. Tofurky would not exist without you.

Mark Machilis, for pioneering work in plant-based foods and for being a sharp, fair businessman.

Karen Goodwin, for being the most brilliant co-packer of foods the world has ever known.

Heather Doyle, for cutting-edge customer service and for being a vegan visionary.

Alan Darer and Mercy for Animals, for suggesting that a book about the search for the wild Tofurky might have legs, even though as a vegan creation it has no actual legs.

Jean Nesterak, for endless sacrifice, friendship, and proving once and for all that English is the best major ever.

Wes Braun, for his keen eye, wit, and graphic ability making Tofurky shine in this world.

Jaime Athos, for being the sharpest knife in the drawer and for carrying on the Tofurky vision so powerfully.

Rachel Perman, for being our north star, forever reminding us of why we are in business.

Gene Baur, for creating a transformative space where animals are friends, not food.

Susie Coston, for showing me the intricate personalities of farm animals that led me to veganism.

Jo-Anne MacArthur, for generously sharing all those photos that touch so many hearts.

Lisa Shapiro, for your contagious, righteous, and uncompromising love of all animals.

Mark Moore, for your enthusiasm and for trail-blazing Tofurky products into the grocery channel.

James Curley, Cindy Wong, and Robin Baumer, for bringing order, stability, and magic to Tofurky sales.

Erin Ransom, for herding all the stray Tofurky marketing elements into a cohesive and sparkling brand.

Beth and Daniel Redwood, for both being compassionate advocates and brilliant teachers, songsters, and photographers.

George Diaz, for excellent work helping to get the book ball rolling.

Peter McGuigan, Mark Weinstein, Scott Waxman, and Emily Hillebrand, for their enthusiasm, wit, and guidance through the book maze.

Carmen Jeronimo, Filiberta Bahena, Hilda Medina, Maria Lupe Martinez, Maricela Rodriguez, Margarita Vargas, Martha Rodriguez, Miguel Villafana, Octavio Delgado Gonzaga, Olga Robledo, Ramona Lachino, and Rosevelt Ocampo, for being outstanding human beings and for years of dedication and hard, hard work making Tofurky products.

Greg Place, for his wise understandings of both people and machines.

Ron Walters, Mandy McGowan, and Tofurky Logistics, for years of excellence and customer service.

Andy Kunkler, for taking financial accounting and organization to the next level and beyond.

Bill Shurtleff, for being a soy foods visionary, historian, cheerleader, and invaluable resource for me and so many others over the years.

Marcia Walker and Tofurky R&D and QA, for endless innovation and a tireless commitment to safety and quality.

Emilia Leese, for her powerful writing, proofreading skills, and deep insights into veganism.

Steve Richardson, for being the best writer, editor, and quarry master in the world. If you want to write a book, hire this man!

Rosie Lundquist, for her quick wit, great pie, and challenging my dream at an early stage that somehow pushed me forward. I think she would be surprised to find so much Tofurky being eaten throughout the Midwest and in all corners of the now not-so-meat-centric world.

At this point, I'm standing on so many shoulders that it's hard to keep track of them all. If you helped to shoulder Turtle Island Foods, The Tofurky Company, or this book into the world and aren't mentioned here, it's an oversight, and I apologize. Sincerely. As I said at the beginning of the book, this would be a sad story without every one of you helping to make it work out so well.

ABOUT THE AUTHOR

(Beth Lily Redwood)

SETH TIBBOTT is the Founder and Chairman of The Tofurky Company and its CEO of thirty-five years. He isn't a former Wharton whiz kid or stock junky; in fact, he was an idealistic hippie with no business acumen living in a treehouse when he conceived the idea of bringing healthy, eco-friendly, tasty protein to the world. Nearly forty years later, using his unconventional approach to business paired with his faith in his products and a deep belief in environmental causes, he has transformed the $2,500 startup into a family-owned global brand worth over $100 million. He lives in Trout Lake, Washington.

INDEX